BLESSABLE

7 HABITS OF PEOPLE BLESSED BY GOD

DR. THIEN H. DOAN

WWW.THIENDOAN.NET

PRAISE AND REVIEWS

The following are praise and reviews for Dr. Thien Doan's best-selling book, *The LIFE Path*.

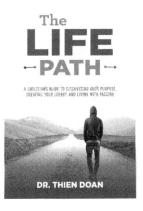

Available on Amazon

The best thing I have read in a long time!

— B. Doud

A must read for everyone that finds himself in the crossroads of life.

— M. Sevillano

I read this book in one sitting. It is both Biblical and practical. I appreciate the several useful tips and recommendations throughout the book for finding and achieving my own personal life path. Thien writes with passion, intelligence and a refreshing sense of humor. I recommend this book to anyone interested in becoming all that God has created them to be.

— Dr. Buddy Mendez, PhD

Love the down to earth style of writing. The principles outlined here are easily adaptable to my personal life and can move us from where we are to where we want to be. Real. Simple. Practical.

— C.M. Simmons

Dr. Doan has written an approachable, concise, and helpful book. The steps forward are clear after you read this book and I highly recommend you read and follow.

— T. Ortho

Engaging & insightful. I especially appreciate how this well-credentialed author chooses not to use 'impressive' language, but is rather plain-spoken & to the point. Refreshing.

— J. COMFORT

The beauty of this book is you can take from it what works for you and apply it to your life.

— R. MONTER

Refreshingly raw... Very insightful and gives a great deal of wisdom with practical application.

— R. TITUS

I feel like I am drifting in life right now and this book has helped me to get focused and apply some practical steps to get back on track.

— S. NGUYEN

I can say this book gave me the answers that I've been waiting for years to hear so I can do what God has called me to do in ministry. I just love the straight forwardness and to the straight to point in his teaching style, I simply love it.

— S. YANCEY-STEWART

Thien's book is simply fabulous... I am a Christian and I have found this book to be a fantastic self-searching document filled with scriptural truths superimposed on references from day-to-day occurrences and dramas.

— A.B. FRIDAY

I love books on purpose, guidance, and clarity. Dr. Doan does an excellent job at communicating how to get clarity on your life path and take action. This book is packed with Scripture, but he is also not afraid to use other elements to help his point - such as the hero journey structure, and other self-improvement models that have truly helped people step into their unique calling.

— D. RAMOS

This book is awesome! Who would've thought a Christian book can have sense of humor, wit, AND wisdom all in one?! This book is a very easy read and a page turner...

The way the book was written is very refreshing and actually fun to read, all the while can change your life from a wandering lifestyle to a purposeful and intentional one. Definitely recommend it to others.

— G.J. Lee

If you are a millennial and wandering, this book is for you. Thien creates systems that are easy and practical to follow. He creates this beautiful bridge between the inspiration passion of the millennial and the committed consistent drive of the generation that came before.

He teaches you not only what to do but how to create a system of life that can best maximize your potential. I totally recommend this book to any new grad and hopeless wanderers out there.

— T. Nguyen

CONTENTS

INTRODUCTION

It was a dark and stormy night... well, not really. But it felt like it inside my soul. I was experiencing what St. John of the Cross called the *dark night of the soul.*

I was frustrated with myself and angry with God. I couldn't even pray.

I was visiting Little Rock, Arkansas for the first time in years. Little Rock holds a special place in my heart. My wife and I lived there for only a year while we got trained to plant churches. We have so many good memories of our time there.

After leaving Little Rock, we moved to Long Beach, California to plant churches. It was our vision to reach our city with a diverse family of churches. Within a few years, we planted two little churches.

Our two churches represented two demographic extremes of our city. Our downtown congregation served the urban poor. Our second congregation served the wealthy neighborhoods of Belmont Shore and Naples Island. We had a vision of becoming a family of faith made up of people from every ethnic and socio-economic stratum.

I was asked to come back to Little Rock for a speaking engagement. I spoke to a crowd of several thousand people about what God was doing in the two churches that I planted and led. I shared about the lives that God was changing and how God was using us to make a difference in our city.

Later that afternoon, I drove to one of my favorite places in Little Rock. When I lived there, I took my family hiking at Pinnacle Mountain State Park. It brought back so many good memories. They don't call Arkansas *The Natural State* for nothing. It's just beautiful.

Although the scenery was beautiful, what was going on in my soul was not. The last time I hiked that trail, I was a young, enthusiastic, and optimistic pastor eager to change the world. This time, I hiked the trail as an older, beaten up, and discouraged grizzled vet of one too many ministry wars.

Planting churches and doing ministry in our two unique contexts was much harder than I imagined. Everything was hard. There were no easy gains. We had to scratch and claw for every little bit of progress.

My wife and I made innumerable sacrifices in pursuit of this calling from God. There were even a few months where the church couldn't pay us a salary and we had to cash out our retirement to pay bills. On top of all this, my wife got pregnant with our third child and had severe complications with the pregnancy. She had to endure six surgeries during the pregnancy. I felt we had suffered enough. Now I thought God owed me.

But that wasn't the thing that really frustrated me. Even though the stories about the lives we impacted were true, I knew that when I got back home I had to shut down one of our two churches. I think I was going through the entire Kubler-Ross cycle of grief all at once. This was a church that my wife and I sacrificed for. Now I had to close it down because it wasn't viable and self-sustaining.

Not too many people will experience the pain of closing down a church. I guess it's a similar emotion to closing down a family business. But one difference is that I was certain that God had called me to this work. I believed that He was going to bless the work of my hands and the churches would thrive. It was an assignment that I believed God has personally called me to. And I gave it my all and did my best to obey.

I kept my end of the bargain, but God wasn't keeping up His. I felt God let me down. I felt abandoned.

As I hiked along that familiar trail, my anger and emotions overwhelmed me. I started shouting my frustrations to God out loud.

What did I do to deserve this? Are you punishing me? You're blessing other people. Why aren't you blessing me? Why are you withholding your blessing from me? Why are you so stingy and cheap?

When are you going to fix this? It's all your fault! You got me into this. You'd better fix it.

Yeah, I know. It was immature and lacking perspective. But that was what was in my heart. I was angry and frustrated. In my mind, God was holding out on me. He was being a cheap miser, hoarding the good stuff for Himself to use on a rainy day.

God didn't answer my questions that day. Actually, I don't think God has ever answered any of my questions that start with "Why."

Have you ever felt this way? I think you can relate, can't you? Maybe not about the pain of closing down a church. But you're probably familiar with wanting God to bless you and your situation and feeling the pain of disappointment when He doesn't.

See if you can relate to any of these scenarios. You want God to bless your marriage. Or your children. Or your business. You ask God to intervene and fix a problem. You pray for God's hand of blessing to bring physical and relational wholeness and healing. But nothing happens. Nothing. The heavens are silent.

God chooses not to bless you. Instead He chooses to withhold His blessing on your life. It would be so easy for Him to open up the floodgates of heaven and rain blessing upon you. But He chooses to not place His hand of blessing on your life. However, it does seem like He is readily blessing other people instead.

I struggled with God over this issue. Yeah, I know that you know how it feels. It's frustrating, right? This is the reason I wanted to try to understand how and why God blesses the people He does.

Through studying the Bible, I gained some insights about God's blessings that encouraged me. So, this is what this book is about. I want to share with you what I learned about how, why, and who God blesses. I believe that these biblical insights and lessons will be helpful and encouraging to you too.

But before we start, let me introduce myself. My name is Thien (it's pronounced "Tee-Inn"). I'm a pastor, husband, father, author, optimistic L.A. Lakers fan, and many other things. But mostly, I'm a Christian.

I wasn't always a follower of Jesus. I was raised in a half-Buddhist and half-Catholic family, which made me fully confused. I learned to appreciate my non-Christian upbringing. I think it's made me a better Christian. I have a different worldview and perspective compared to those that grew up going to church.

I started going to a Baptist church as a teenager to find solace and escape from my tumultuous life at home. I was going through a personal crisis and struggling inside. I would say angry and hurtful things to myself. I blamed myself for things that no child should. So I thought I'd give church a try. What would it hurt?

Overnight, God changed my life. The change was real and tangible. Everyone around me noticed it. God did something special and He got the glory. One time a party-girl from school confided in me that she wanted to kill herself. Even though she was popular, she struggled with depression. She asked me what I did to change my life. I told her about what Jesus did. She gave her life to Jesus and her life was changed too. God used that experience to call me into ministry.

God had a plan for my life. He helped me overcome incredible obstacles and has used me to help a lot of people meanwhile. For that, I'm so grateful. I still can't believe that I have the honor of serving the King of Glory. I've been doing it for two decades and I still love it.

Along the way, I've learned a thing or two about following God. But I had to learn them all the hard way. I struggled and wrestled with God over many issues and years. I failed and made countless mistakes. Through my doubts, despair, and detours, God developed my faith and gave me a message to share.

I paid the dumb tax of discipleship so you don't have to. I learned many lessons about following God which I can show you that will help you grow in your relationship with God. So if you would let me, I want to be Mr. Miyagi and you can be Daniel-San. Let me give you some useful faith advice. Let me show you how you can conquer your enemies, overcome your obstacles, and enjoy God's hand of blessing upon your life.

Are you ready? First lesson: wax my car. Wax on. Wax off.

Just kidding. Let's talk about becoming a person that God wants to bless.

~

Do you want FREE RESOURCES?

Teaching videos
Seminars & Workshops
PDF Downloads
Beta Editions of future books

Check out my website:
www.thiendoan.net

Chapter 1

BLESSED SUPER-CHRISTIANS

Every now and then I bump into these strange people. I call them "Super-Christians." I lived in Arkansas for a year and found out that the South is full of them. I don't see too many of them in Southern California. But they're around here too if you know where to look.

They're the ones that carry those big Bibles to church. The ones with the zippered covers and a dozen multicolored ribbon bookmarks. They're the ones that highlight, underline, and take color-coded notes in their Bibles. They do Bible Study like John Nash from the movie, *A Beautiful Mind*. It's like they're trying to decipher a secret code.

The men wear suits and ties to church. The ladies sport the latest dresses from the *Laura Ingalls Wilder Collection*. Their kids wear the latest Christian T-shirts. I've seen one with a confusing chemistry equation that claims that helium is greater than iodine ($He > i$). I don't get it. (But I didn't do well in chemistry.)

They're not just Christian. They're *Super-Christian.* Comedian Michael Jr. calls these Christians "over-saved." You know who I'm talking about, right? Well, if you don't, I'm probably talking about you. Can I get an Amen?

If you go up to one of these over-saved, *Super-Christians* and ask them, "How are you doing?" They will all say the same thing. Every time. They learn it in the *Super-Christian* orientation manual.

Section I, article 3, it says:

> *When asked, "How are you doing?" the only appropriate reply is to say, "I'm blessed! How are you?"*

"I'm blessed. How are you?" If those words have ever come out of your mouth, you are a *Super-Christian.* Jeff Foxworthy could do a funny comedy bit about *Super-Christians.*

You know you're a *Super-Christian* if...

- You think the Bible questions on Jeopardy are way too easy.
- You ever carried your Bible in an empty casserole dish.
- You say, "I'm blessed" when someone asks you how you're doing.

"I'm blessed." What does that even mean? When a Christian, regular or super, says "I'm blessed," what are they trying to communicate?

Well, that's a hard question to answer. There are many layers to that question.

I've been a pastor for twenty years with Masters and Doctoral degrees in theology and ministry. And I still had to look up the word "blessing" in the Bible Dictionary.

This is how Tyndale defines *blessing*:

> *Blessing generally denotes a bestowal of good. Usually conceived of as material but also denotes the spiritual good brought by the gospel. Often it is contrasted with cursing.*

So, a "blessed" person is someone who received a good gift of material or spiritual value. When a person says, "I'm blessed," they're making a theological statement. They are stating that they believe God has bestowed upon them good gifts of some kind, gifts that they did not earn or even deserve. They believe that God has shown them special favor.

If you listen to the *Dave Ramsey Show*, you'll notice the unique way Dave greets the callers of his radio show. The caller says, "Hi Dave, how are you?"

Because Dave is an *Ultra-Super-Christian*, he always replies, "I'm doing better than I deserve."

That's his unique way of saying, "I'm blessed." Yeah Dave, yes you are. Five New York Times Best-Selling books. An award-winning nationally syndicated radio show. Appearances on Oprah, 60 Minutes, Fox, etc. An international ministry. A great family, white teeth, health, wealth, and prosperity! But that's not all. God is using Dave to make a difference in the lives of millions. Yup, Dave is blessed. (At least he's bald. If he also had good hair, it would be too much to bear.)

I want to be blessed too! Don't you? I want God to use me to make a difference. That's my goal in life. I want my life to matter. That's what I've been pursuing in ministry for the majority of my adult life. Of course a little bit of health, wealth, and prosperity wouldn't hurt either. I want my life to be blessed. Is that so bad? Don't you want to be blessed too?

And I'm not just talking about the "I know I'm saved" and "God has a crown of life in heaven for me" type of blessing. I'm talking about living with an overflowing sense of gratitude for God's special hand of favor on my life. The "open the floodgates of heaven" kind of blessing. Where God blesses you so much you don't have room to contain it all kind. That's the kind of blessing I want. I want my cup to be filled past the point of overflowing. I want to experience what Jesus meant when He said, "I've come to give you life, and life abundantly."

Abundance. Overflow. Floodgates. That's what comes

into my mind when I think of blessing. That's what I want. Don't you?

So how does one become "blessed by God"? That's the million dollar question. Blessing is a gift from God. You don't work for it. No amount of faith or positive thinking or good deeds will guarantee God's blessing. You don't earn gifts. You don't work for blessings. God blesses whom He chooses to bless. It's up to Him to decide how, when, and on whom He will shower His blessings.

But that doesn't mean we don't have a role in being blessed. There is something we can do. If you want to be blessed, you don't have to sit back and wait passively. There's something you can do while you're waiting.

I used to get frustrated at God because I didn't feel like He blessed me enough. I would look around at others with envy and complain to God, "How come you blessed him more than me? That's not fair!"

Have you ever said that to God? I used to think, "That's not fair!" was a compelling argument until I became a parent of three sinners forgiven by Jesus. Now I know that is an accusation only naive and immature people make.

I've learned that if I want to be blessed by God, I have a role to play in it. Now, I'm not suggesting a magical formula to manipulate God into showering me with gifts like some Genie in the Lamp. I'm not advocating a Christianized version of *The Law of Attraction* that the prosperity gospel teaches.

PARENTING AT WALMART

If you want to be a person that is blessed by God, what should you do? Of course, the first thing is to pray and ask God to bless you. That's obvious. But then what? Is that all? Just pray and wait?

It is 100% God's prerogative on whom, when and how much He will bless someone. There's no formula to manipulate God to bless you. The best way I can explain it is with an example from parenthood.

I have three children that I dearly love. It makes me happy and brings me great joy to be able to bless my children. One of my primary *languages of love* is giving gifts. I love to surprise my kids with unexpected gifts. I'm also impulsive and a pushover. This is evident when I take my kids to the store.

The following scenario has occurred more than I would like to admit. My wife sends me to Target or Walmart to get something like toilet paper or dish washing detergent. Then one of my kids begs me to take them with me. They know that I'm a pushover and I like to show love through gift giving. (You know how this story is going to turn out, right?)

As we stroll down the aisle at Walmart, the toy section of the store beckons for my child's attention. There she finds yet another toy, trinket or stuffed animal she can't live without.

"Daddy please?" my baby asks.

I am weak-minded and I fall victim to my child's *Jedi Mind Trick* and this new toy ends up in our shopping cart. I don't mind it.

She's grins, and says, "Thank you! Thank you! You're the best dad in the world!"

I can't help but grin too. Blessing her makes me happy.

On our way to pay for the items, she spots another item that she can't live without. She goes through the same act of asking for that new item with the grin and the "Daddy please?"

At this point, the *Jedi Mind Trick* has worn off and I say, "Honey, really? No. We can't get this. Put it back."

Then without warning, she turns on me. My lovely sweet child, the one with the happy grin morphs into an entitled reality show diva. The one who thinks she has the "best daddy in the world," turns on me right there in front of fifty strangers. She folds her arms, stomps her feet, and shouts in protest, "But why can't I have it? I WANT IT!"

Sometimes, for emphasis, she plunges the knife in my back and twists, saying: "You don't love me! You never get me anything!"

Hmmm, excuse me. Oh no you didn't. What did you say to me?

I try to muster up as much sanctification and Holy Ghost Power as I can. I'm call on God to give me the strength to not lose it. Besides, we're at Walmart and I'm a pastor. I don't want to end up on a YouTube video berating and spanking my child in the store. Although I must admit that public spanking isn't all that unusual at Walmart. (Which is probably why my wife prefers to go to Target.)

I take a deep breath, and I get down on one knee so I am eye to eye with my child.

As calmly as I can, this is what I say:

> *Honey, please listen. I want you to know that I love you with all my heart. I like buying you things because making you happy, makes me happy.*
>
> *But I will not tolerate the way you are acting right now. Not only am I not getting you this second item, I'm going to put the first one back too.*
>
> *Because if I gave you what you want right now, you would think that it was okay for you to act this way. I cannot reward this kind of behavior. Now go put those items back on the shelf.*

I'm not the best parent in the world. But I do know that giving in will lead to something bad later on. Buying her that toy after she threw a tantrum would send the wrong message. That would have given her the impression that there are zero consequences for her bad behavior.

Then my child would grow up to become an unmanageably spoiled brat. Inevitably, she would throw that tantrum again. If that happened on a day I wasn't completely filled with the Holy Spirit, I would lose it and become one of those people performing "inappropriate parental discipline" at Walmart. Someone would catch me on video and put it on YouTube. It would cause a scandal and I would get fired from my church. I would have to go and find a new job. But because I have two non-marketable theology degrees, the only job I can find is in the telemarketing department at a vacation timeshare company. I would have to call you during your dinner time and then you would probably hang up on me. And neither of us wants that to happen. It's just not worth it.

I really don't want to become a telemarketer. So that's why I don't buy my daughter what she wants when she is misbehaving. That makes sense, right? You have to admit, I have a dizzying intellect.

Behaviorist call it *positive reinforcement*. You reward only the behavior that you want to see repeated. You don't even have to punish bad behavior. You just refuse to reward it, and only reward the good behavior. Pretty soon, your child would get it. She will know that the only way to get a new *Disney Tsum Tsum* stuffy is to kiss up to dad and compliment him on his weight loss, because that is a behavior dad wants repeated.

This is such a simple concept that even my Golden Retriever understands it. If my dog wants me to reward her with a treat, she better not pee on the rug. Pee on the rug; no reward. No pee; it's time for Milk Bones! Simple, right? This concept of *positive reinforcement* is so obvious in our own households. Why can't we see it is also the primary pattern of how God teaches us?

I hear Christians complain about their frustration with God all the time. They wonder why God hasn't answered their prayers. They don't receive the blessing, abundance, or prosperity they hoped for. They are impatient and frustrated and say immature, stupid things like, "Well, I'm not sure I can trust God."

Forgive me if I am being too harsh. But I want to grab that person and shake them vigorously to get their attention.

Then I would shout in their face:

> *Why in the world would you think God would want to bless you right now? You are acting like an impatient, ungrateful, spoiled brat! God is not going to bless that. If you want to be blessed, then you better make yourself blessable!*

So, in a few words, this is the premise of this book:

> *God blesses a person who is blessable. God does not bless a person who is unblessable.*

PROMISE AND PREMISE

I'm not sure if *blessable* is already a word. If not, I'm going to copyright and trademark it and put it on some mugs and T-shirts (#blessable). A *blessable* person is someone that God is more likely to bless. An *unblessable* person is someone that God is less likely to bless. If this is true, and you want to be blessed by God, then you might as well work on making yourself as *blessable* as you can.

Of course, there are exceptions and outliers to this premise. But that statement is generally true. Though we can point out examples where God seems to shower His blessings at random, He is not random at all. The Bible says that God is looking for certain kinds of people to bless.

2 Chronicles 16:9 says:

> *For the eyes of the LORD run to and fro throughout the whole earth, to give strong support to those whose heart is blameless toward Him.*

God is looking for people to bless. He wants to give "strong support" to specific people. In Hebrew that verse says that God wants to "show Himself as strong" to certain people. Now that's a good definition of being blessed. I want to be one of those people that God would come to and show His strong support in my life and endeavors. I want to be able to see God show Himself as strong on my behalf. Don't you?

But to whom does God give His "strong support"? He is searching throughout the earth for people "whose heart is blameless toward Him." Those are the people that He's going to bless. He's going to bless those people because they are *blessable*.

Not only is this concept biblically consistent, it's also logical and practical. So, what should you do if you want to be blessed by God? Stop doing nothing. Stop waiting passively for God to choose you. Instead, you should work on making yourself less *unblessable*, and more *blessable*.

I like to be practical. Good theology without good practice is as useful as a pork sandwich at a Jewish BBQ. It's wasted.

So, let's get practical. I want to show you how to become *blessable*. I want to show you seven character qualities that will make you more of a person that God is more likely to bless. I want to help you develop these character qualities in your life. I'll even suggest seven habits that will help you become more of a *blessable* person.

I'm not saying that if you do these things it will guarantee that God will bless you. It's up to God who He decides to bless. This is not a health, wealth, and prosperity manual. This is not a way to manipulate God into helping you roll like John Gotti in a new Bugatti with some fine hotties. Sorry, but you're going to have to put away your Jabez prayer shawl. We're not going to use it.

This book is about making deliberate choices. Choices to develop your character and becoming someone that God is more likely to bless.

There's nothing you can do to make God bless you. He's

not a cosmic vending machine in the sky, or your own personal Genie in the Lamp.

While you can't force God to bless you, you can make yourself into someone that God is more likely to bless. That's the goal of this book. I want to help you become more *blessable*.

Chapter 2
DON'T CALL SAUL

I've always had this compelling desire in my heart to make a difference. From an early age, I had a vision that God was going to use me in a special way. I want to be someone that God uses to make a difference. I want my life to matter. Don't you?

Most people want to be "successful," whatever that means. Usually it includes money and power. Many pursue success with abandon. As a deer pants for streams of water, so their soul yearns for success. They sacrifice and strive for this goal.

But what does earthly "success" bring you?

Universities and hospitals have buildings named after successful people. Imagine you were wildly successful and wealthy and you didn't want to leave your money to your rotten kids. You might donate your millions to a college or hospital. In return that institution would name a building after you in your honor.

The college that I went to has a building called Sutherland Hall. I'm not sure who Mr. Sutherland was, but he probably was wildly successful. Perhaps it was Mr. Kiefer Sutherland, but I doubt Jack Bauer went to Bible College. (I know, I used this joke before in another book, but it's still funny.)

Chasing success is much like a kid chasing bubbles in the sky. When he thinks he has caught a bubble, he open his hands and there is nothing there.

Rather than seeking to become "successful," it is so much better to become "significant." In my previous book, *The LIFE Path,* I discussed the importance of leaving a good legacy. What is the legacy of a successful person? Success may get your name on a building one day. But significance gets your name written on the hearts of people that you've impacted. Success is about building your resume. But significance is about building your legacy.

The Bible is full of stories of significant people. People who made a difference in their day. I want to spend some time looking at the life of one of the most significant people in the whole Bible, King David.

David was the second king of Israel. God blessed David in so many ways. In the following chapters, we'll take a closer look at his life and find out what made him so *bless-able.* Then we'll compare it with Israel's first king, the not-so-blessed King Saul.

Saul was the very first king of Israel and he wasn't a very good guy. Don't get him confused with the Saul in the

New Testament who became the Apostle Paul. There's about a thousand years that separates those two Bible characters.

The people of Israel demanded a king and they choose Saul. Why did they choose Saul? Was he a spiritual leader? Did he have strong moral character? Nope.

What would you look for in a leader? That's still a relevant question. That's the question our nation hotly debates during every election cycle.

What do people look for in their leaders? He (or she) needs to be tall, charismatic, well-spoken, have unique strengths or skills. And most importantly, he needs to have the ability to produce results!

What qualities do American voters look for in their leaders? Here's the top three:

1. Image
2. Ability
3. Results

The more things change, the more they stay the same. The Israelites looked for the same characteristics to select their commander in chief. And the person that fit the bill was a guy named Saul.

Saul checked all the boxes for the Israelites. He was the tallest, strongest, most charismatic warrior in the whole land. If anyone would be able to get some results and "Make Israel Great Again!" it was the newly crowned King Saul.

But, as the old adage says, "Be careful what you wish for, you might actually get it."

Saul was full of charisma and he looked the part. He was a tall, dark, strong and handsome warrior. He was the middle-eastern equivalent to Tom Brady. The quintessential captain of the football team. He was a strong warrior, skilled in battle. And he could get some results, too. The people believed he could lead Israel to defeat their enemies in battle.

They were looking for a person of charisma, strength and results. But they ignored his character. Saul was a terrible leader. His downfall was not his lack of strength, but his lack of character.

Saul's lack of character lead to devastating circumstances for the nation of Israel. His narcissistic pride plagued him. He led the nation with a lack of integrity. He was rash and impatient in his decisions. And when he failed, he was too prideful and self-absorbed to own up to his mistakes, and then tried to cover them up or blame others.

Due to his lack of character, God had to remove Saul as the King of Israel. God removed His hand of blessing from Saul because of his lack of character. His lack of character made him *unblessable*. The Bible even said that God regretted making Saul the King of Israel.

This should serve as a lesson for us on what to look for in a leader to follow. I want to highlight some warning signs of a bad leader. Think about these signs the next time you have two job offers. Be careful which boss you choose to work for. If you see these warning signs in one of your potential bosses, choose the other opportunity. If you're looking for a new church to attend, and you see these warning signs in the pastor, keep looking.

These warning signs can also serve as a mirror in which we evaluate ourselves. If you see any of these warning signs in your own life, it's time to reevaluate and make a course correction.

WHAT GOD LOOKS FOR

If you were looking for an opposite to Saul, you would find David. Saul was a tall and strong warrior. David was a young, weak, indie musician and poet from a poor sheep farming family. Today, you would find him working part-time as a barista at Starbucks. Or hosting spoken word performances and open mic nights at the local hipster hangout. He was the youngest and the smallest in his own family. He would have been voted, "Least Likely to Become King."

David is most famous for his victorious battle with the Philistine giant. He defeated Goliath on his way to becoming the greatest king in Israel's history. His story is interesting and complex.

Outside of Jesus, David is arguably the most significant person in the whole Bible. There are more chapters written about David than any other person. David has 66 chapters of the Bible written about him in the Old Testament. And there are an addition 59 references to David in the New Testament. That dwarfs any of the other Bible characters. By comparison, Abraham has only 14 chapters devoted to him. Joseph also has 14 chapters, Jacob has 11, and Elijah has 10.

David lived during a very troubled time in the history of the Nation of Israel. He lived around the year 1000 BC, after the "Time of the Judges." This was a lawless time where "everyone did what was right in his own eyes." The High Priest's sons were sinful and corrupt. The Prophet Samuel's sons were also disobedient to God.

The people lost confidence in their spiritual leaders and did the unthinkable. They demanded a human king. They didn't want to be led by God's spiritual leaders anymore.

Israel choose Saul to be their king for his charisma, strength and ability to win a battle. They wanted a leader, a strong king who would lead them to defeat their enemies on the battlefield.

Saul oozed with strength and competence. But he lacked character. And character is so much more important than competence. You can always teach someone to grow in competence and skill, but character comes from the state of your soul.

This concept is so simple and clear. Yet we ignore it all the time. It doesn't seem as though we value character much these days.

When was the last time you were asked character questions in a job interview? Your potential boss doesn't seem to care if you are a person of good character. They only want to know if you can get the job done and meet the quarterly goals.

This may be how it's done in business, but this is not how it is done in the Kingdom of God. God cares very much about your character, and very little about your level of competence. It seems that God actually goes out of His way to choose unlikely people. He chooses those who are very low in competence to bless and promote to prominence. Why? They are people of high character.

Blessable people are people of high character. Think about that. Why would God want to bless someone of low character? God regularly blesses and promotes people of high character even if they have zero experience. God values character far more than competency. He passes over a person with high competency and low character every time.

In comparing King Saul and King David, we'll see a clear contrast. Saul had all the competency, skill and experience to lead others. David was a young shepherd boy who had a heart for God. In God's eyes, it was a clear decision of who to bless. You bless the person with good character. Why? Because good character makes you *blessable*. Bad character makes you *unblessable*.

So how do we become *blessable* people of good character? There are at least seven character traits that David possessed that Saul did not. These were the reasons that

God chose David. Even today, these are the seven character traits God is looking for in the person He wants to bless.

PREVIEW

In the following chapters, we will compare the life and character of King Saul with King David. It was David's character that made him a *blessable* person. And it was Saul's lack of character that made him an *unblessable* person.

When you look at David's life, you'll see why God blessed him so much. He was a man of strong moral character and spirituality.

David's strength of character could be seen in seven areas:

1. A Heart for God
2. Humility
3. Integrity
4. Faithfulness
5. Patience
6. Repentance
7. Gratitude

We know that David was a unique person who played special role in the plan of God. None of us are David. God used him in a special way. Please understand that I am not saying that if we do what David did, God will bless us in the same way He blessed David. There was and will only ever be one David.

But I do believe that we can learn a lot from David's example about living a *blessable* life. What made David *blessable* was his character, not his giftedness. So, let's allow David to teach us how we can become *blessable* people of high character.

Chapter 3

A HEART FOR GOD

BLESSABLE CHARACTERISTIC #1

THE PRIDEFULNESS OF SAUL

Everything changed for King Saul. He's made many terrible decisions but this one was the most tragic. It was subtle, almost unnoticed by others. But it's one of the most heartbreaking stories in the Bible.

Saul was the first king of Israel. He was chosen by the people because he was a skilled and strong warrior. He was their greatest warrior and represented their best chance to win on the battlefield against their enemies.

Early in his career, God was with Saul. God blessed Saul. God's special presence and anointing was with King Saul. But that all changed in a moment.

Israel's army was preparing to battle their nemesis, the Philistines. King Saul waited with 2,000 of Israel's best soldiers for the Prophet Samuel to come and offer a sacrifice to God and ask for blessing before they go off into battle. Saul didn't like waiting and grew impatient.

So he decided not to wait for Samuel to offer the sacrifices. He did something that was strictly forbidden in Old Testament law and committed the most grievous sin possible. He decided to offer the sacrifices to God himself. This was a grave sin. Offering sacrifices was a job reserved only for priests or prophets. Saul was a warrior with much blood on his hands. This was a grave sin.

He was foolish, impatient, arrogant, and impulsive. A man of with low character. It was at this very moment God removed His hand of blessing from Saul. God could no longer bless Saul because his lack of character and the resultant bad decisions made him *unblessable*.

The Prophet Samuel told him, "But now your kingdom will not continue. The Lord has sought out a man after his own heart..." (1 Samuel 13:14).

This was the account of the moment when God stopped blessing King Saul. One moment he was blessed and anointed by God. The next he was *unblessable*. This is the ultimate tragedy. Saul had God's hand of blessing upon his life. Then he completely blew it. He tested God's patience past its limits, forcing God to stop blessing Saul. God removed His blessing upon Saul because of his lack of character. Instead, God chose to bless a young shepherd boy named David.

The people wanted Saul for his leadership ability and warrior skills. But God wanted "a man after his own heart."

You've heard it said, "You are what you eat." Theologically, it could be said, "You become what you love." David was blessed because of what was inside his heart. God blessed David because of his character.

SEEKING HIS HEART OR HIS HAND

The Bible says God chose to bless David because he was a person *after God's heart.* What does that mean? What does it look like to be a person *after God's heart?* It's a person who is pursuing a relationship with God, one that is passionately following and seeking to honor God.

Sometimes we misunderstand what it means to seek God. People seek God for many reasons. But it's easy to confuse seeking God's heart with seeking God's hand. When we go to God to ask Him to do stuff for us, that is seeking His hand. That's a person who is trying to use and manipulate God as a means to an end. Seeking God's hand is different than seeking God's heart.

Many people today go to church, read the Bible, and pray in pursuit of something other than God. They do their religious activities in pursuit of something else. They think that through these activities, they can gain blessing from God. They see God as some sort of divine vending machine from which they get what they ultimately want.

They read the Bible to find the secrets to a happy life, or keys to abundance. They pray for material and financial blessings. They make sincere faith declarations. They fully believe that God will send a flood of blessing their way. There is a danger to this way of thinking.

WHAT DID YOU BRING ME?

Let me try to explain the difference. I love my family and enjoy being present with them. However, there have been seasons when I had to travel and be away from home for extended periods of time. I feel guilty being away from my wife and three kids, so I always bring home gifts for each person from my trips.

Usually I find some cheap trinkets or local treats from the Chotsky store. My youngest has an impressive little collection of shot glasses that I picked up at airport stores from exotic locations such as Reno and Little Rock. Sometimes she uses them for pretend tea parties with her dolls and stuffed animals. (I don't have the heart to tell her that I think her teddy is an alcoholic and he's not drinking tea, but shots of Jack.)

When I come home from a trip, my kids line up and greet me at the door with hugs and kisses.

"Daddy has a surprise for you," I say, "I bought you some gifts. Now close your eyes."

With their eyes closed, I hand each their gifts. They can barely contain their giddiness. They receive my gifts with joy and gratitude.

"O thanks Daddy! You're the best! I love you, Daddy!"

I'm elated, and I don't feel like such a bad father anymore.

Even when my travel schedule got busier, I would still keep up this habit. I always buy gifts to "surprise" my kids upon my return. Of course, it's no longer a surprise but has become an expectation.

Over time, something changes. Upon arriving at home, my kids would still line up at the door to greet me. But now, they don't greet me with hugs and kisses anymore. They stand there at the door with their eyes closed and hands extended and say, "Daddy, Daddy, what did you get me?"

"Hmmm," I wonder to myself, "Where did the hugs and kisses go?"

Somewhere my kids started seeing me as "the guy who brings us gifts from far off places." They seem to care more about the gifts in their father's hand than his heart. I wonder how they would respond if I stopped bringing presents home. Would they still be as excited to see me if I didn't give them anything?

This is how many Christians begin to see God. Somewhere along the journey, we stop pursuing God because we want a relationship with Him. But we come to God to see if He has any gifts He would like to give us.

If you want to assess where your heart is, listen to what you pray for when you are alone. What are you pursuing? What does your heart's desire cry out and ache for? What do you hope for? What thing, that if God gave you, would bring happiness to your soul? What thing, that if God does not give you, will devastate you? The answers to those questions will reveal where you heart is. It will show you how God-centered you are. And if you're seeking God's hand or His heart.

DAVID'S ONE DESIRE

David's heart was different than Saul's. You can hear it in his prayers. David's prayers reveal the passion of his heart. They reveal that he was a man after God's own heart. David pursued and longed for God Himself, not the things that God could give him.

Psalm 27 is a prayer that David wrote during a dark time in his life. He was alone. His enemies were seeking to kill him. He had to hide out in the dark caves in the Judean desert. But David didn't pray for deliverance, justice, or even blessing. David's sincere and heartfelt prayer reveals that his greatest desire was to be near to God.

Psalm 27:4 says,

> *One thing have I asked of the Lord, that will I seek after: that I may dwell in the house of the Lord all the days of my life, to gaze upon the beauty of the Lord and to inquire in his temple.*

Let me put David's prayer into my own words:

> *Lord, there is only one thing that I want. This is the one thing*

that I desire. This is the one thing that I am pursuing and seeking. I'm not asking for justice, deliverance or even your blessing.

The only thing that I want is to be able to be close to you all the days of my life. I want to be able to see you face to face. I want to be able to go into your presence at any hour. I want to be able to have the access to run up to you and ask you any question that is on my heart. Lord, the only thing I desire is you.

That's the prayer of a person who is seeking God's heart. And God is looking for such people to bless.

If you want to be a person that God can use, do you have to be gifted and talented? No, but you do have to have a heart after God. That's what David had going for himself.

A ME-CENTERED LIFE

King Saul was not a God-centered person. Saul was a Saul-centered person. Everything he did, he did for himself. His self-centeredness was clearly seen in everything that he did and the decisions he made. Even when he lead the army of Israel valiantly in battle, he didn't do it for God. He did it for his own honor and glory.

Once, when returning from a major victory, Saul didn't get the love and recognition he thought he deserved. At the victory parade, the people shouted, "Saul killed his thousands, but David his ten-thousands." When Saul heard that, he absolutely lost his mind!

Saul said to himself, "They have ascribed to David ten-thousands, and to me they have ascribed thousands, and what more can he have but the kingdom?" The Bible says that from that moment on, "Saul eyed David" suspiciously (1 Samuel 18:6-9). He couldn't handle the idea that the people loved and respected someone else. He could not bear the thought of sharing the spotlight with anyone else. He was, as most self-centered people are, deeply insecure with himself.

The Bible says that Saul's anger and jealousy opened his heart up for a "harmful spirit" to enter. The very next day, Saul tried to kill David with a spear. His self-centeredness lead to insecurity, then to jealousy, and then to murderous intent. This always results in suspicion, broken relationships, and sin.

One telling verse is 1 Samuel 18:22, which says,

> *"Saul was afraid of David because the Lord was with him but had departed from Saul."*

What jumps out is that Saul knew God removed His hand of blessing and started blessing David instead. This was something obvious to Saul, and probably obvious to others as well. Losing God's blessing scared Saul, but it didn't change him. Instead of trying to regain God's favor,

Saul continued down this dark road of pride, anger, and hostility.

In contrast to Saul's self-centeredness is David who was God-centered. It is obvious why God removed His hand of blessing from Saul and placed His hand of blessing on the young, humble David.

God doesn't bless self-centered people. God blesses humble people who have a heart after His own heart. So what does this mean for us?

If you want to grow to become more of a God-centered person like David was, I would suggest a good place to start is to read the Psalms. The Psalms are a collection of 150 poems, prayers, and songs written primarily by David. The Psalms represented the most intimate thoughts and heart's cry of a man who pursued God.

HEALTHY AND FRUITFUL

In Psalm 1, David pens one of the most beautiful poems in the Scripture. It describes the life of a *blessable* person.

In Psalm 1:3 says,

> *He is like a tree planted by streams of water, which yields its fruit in season, whose leaf does not wither. All that he does prospers.*

That is such a descriptive picture of a blessed life. I live in Orange County, Southern California. The county is named for the miles and miles of orange orchards that were here before Disneyland and urban development took over. But the soil and the climate is still very much suited for citrus fruit to thrive in your backyard.

I remember the orange, lemon, and tangerine trees at my childhood home. They were healthy, strong, and abundantly fruitful. It is amazing how much fruit one little tree can produce. But even a healthy tree doesn't produce fruit all year around.

As Psalm 1:3 states, "it yields its fruit in season." Even a blessed life does not experience fruitfulness at every season. Even in SoCal, there's no fruit in the winter months. It only has fruit during its appointed time of the year. That's how it is with God's blessing.

So many faithful believers cry out in doubt and despair during the winter months of their souls because of the lack of "fruit" in their lives. They must think being blessed means never experiencing lack or hardship, that blessing should be experienced continuously and unceasingly. That is not so.

Think about it this way. In winter, when there is no fruit on the orange tree, is it still a healthy tree? Of course, it is. You may ask, "Well, if it was healthy, why don't I see any fruit on the tree?" The answer is obvious. It's not the season for fruit.

Just because you don't see the outward signs of growth and

blessing, it doesn't mean that nothing is happening. In China, the giant bamboo can grow up to one foot in a single day. That is amazing! But it doesn't actually happen overnight. Before the giant bamboo can grow upward, it needs to send its roots out into the soil and gather its nutrients. It takes the giant bamboo four years to create the necessary root system before it starts to send its shoots up towards the sky. What looks like overnight explosive growth took four years in the making.

So even the blessed life will not have fruit all the time. But that tree is still healthy and strong. Psalm 1:3 says, "it yields its fruit in season, and whose leaf does not wither." There it is. That's the sign of health and life. If you want to see a blessed person, don't just look for the fruit of blessing. Look for the healthiness of the tree. Don't only look for oranges. Look to see if the leaves are still green.

That healthy tree is a picture of the life of a *blessable* person. He is healthy and strong even in winter, and fruitful during the harvest season. The obvious next question is, "How do I become like that tree? How do I become *blessable?*"

Psalm 1:2 says,

> But his delight is in the law of the Lord, and on his law he meditates day and night.

The word "law" can be translated "instruction" or

"teachings." This is telling us that a blessable person does two things:

1. Delights in the Word of God
2. Meditates continuously on God's Word

Let's talk about what those two actions would look like in your life.

1. Delights in God's Word

What does it mean to *delight* in something? I don't use that word "delight" much in my daily vocabulary. *Deee-Lite* was a terrible music group that produced a funky, psychedelic one-hit-wonder in the early 90s called *Groove is in the Heart*. I picture an old British lady drinking tea from a floral cup saying, "O what a delight" when she got good news.

The word "delight" is a noun and a verb. The noun means "something that gives great pleasure or enjoyment." The origins of the word from the Latin root "delectare" where we get the cognates "delectable" and "delicious."

So, what does it mean when we say a *blessable* person "delights in God's Word"? It means that they find God's Word "delicious" to their soul. The Prophet Jeremiah thought God's Word was delicious to his soul.

In Jeremiah 15:16, he says,

When I discovered your words, I devoured them. They are my joy and my heart's delight... (NLT)

The Prophet Ezekiel describes how he also found God's Word to be richly satisfying.

Ezekiel 3:3 says,

And he said to me, "Son of man, feed your belly with this scroll that I give you and fill your stomach with it." Then I ate it, and it was in my mouth as sweet as honey.

David describes the delectable and sweet taste of God's Word to his soul.

In Psalm 119:103, he says,

How sweet are your words to my taste, sweeter than honey to my mouth!

David loved God's Word so much he wrote Psalm 119 as a "love song" to show his appreciation for the Word of God. It seems like David had a lot to say about his love for Scripture because Psalm 119 happens to be the longest chapter in the whole Bible with 176 verses!

Yes, you can say David found delight in God's Word. The question is "Do you?" I'm not asking if you know God's

Word. I'm not asking if you read the Bible. Or how many verses you know by heart.

I'm asking, do you delight and take pleasure in God's Word? Does it bring joy and pleasure to your heart? Is the Bible sweet to your taste? Or is it cough medicine that you have to swallow fast because it's good for you? No one delights in cough medicine. It's a necessary evil.

If I'm honest, I'll have to admit that there have been seasons when I thought God's Word was cough medicine. I knew I needed it. But I hated the taste. So I swallowed it as fast as I could hoping it would help me somehow. Believe me, I did not experience much of God's blessings in those seasons. If that's how you see God's Word, you won't either.

2. Meditates on God's Word

Psalm 1:2 also says a *blessable* person "meditates day and night" on God's Word. What does it mean to meditate? And do I have to do it day and night?

When most people think of meditation they envision a Buddhist monk or a yoga instructor. However, those two examples are very different from the meditation the Bible prescribes.

The Buddhist monk or yoga instructor will tell you to meditate by quieting yourself. Then find a relaxing position and empty your mind of all your thoughts.

I know what you're thinking. "That's weird. I can't sit still and empty my thoughts. And I certainly can't do that day and night. I got a job and kids to take care of!"

Relax. When the Bible talks about meditation it is not talking about emptying your mind at all. Actually, it's telling us to do the opposite.

The Hebrew word for meditate is "hagah." The Bible uses that funny word 25 separate times in a variety of contexts. That word is also translated as to mutter, speak, imagine, devise, study, and discuss. In a few instances "hagah" is also translated as "to growl, moan, or mourn."

How the Bible describes the act of meditation is very different from how we normally think of meditation. Imagine going into a yoga class and the instructor says, "Let's spend a moment in meditation." Immediately, you start talking, discussing, moaning and growling. They would ask you to leave pretty quickly. What I'm saying is that Christian meditation is different.

Christian meditation is an active mental process, not a clearing of your mind. It is actively wrestling with an idea in your head. I heard Pastor Rick Warren explain meditation with the word "ruminate." It's not a pretty picture but it's a descriptive one that has stuck with me for years.

The literal meaning of "ruminate" refers to the action that a cow goes about in digesting its food. You may know that a cow has multiple stomachs and processes its food continuously. One of the cow's stomach chambers is called the "rumin." When a cow eats grass, the grass goes into one chamber of its stomach to be partially digested. Then after a little while, the cow burps the partially digested grass (called "cud") back up into its mouth. It chews it for a while longer before swallowing it again. The cud then goes back into a different part of its digestive tract to be fully broken down. It takes about 3 days for a cow to digest the food it eats.

This process takes so long because it is trying to extract as much nutrients from the grass as it can. This makes sense because grass isn't exactly rich in nutrients. If you think about it, this is a miraculous process. In only 3 days' time, this glorious animal miraculously turns grass into steak and milk! That's a miracle. God is good! All the time! Can I get an Amen? (BTW, If you said "Amen" out loud, you're definitely a *Super-Christian*.)

Sorry for the lengthy descriptive biological explanation. According to Pastor Rick, the cow's digestive process is a good analogy for Christian meditation. When you meditate on God's Word, you are recalling something you read or heard from the Bible back into your mind. Then you think about it. You ponder it. You even discuss it with yourself or with God in your prayers. What you are doing is "ruminating" on God's Word.

A lot of people don't think they can meditate. Believe it or not, you already meditate continuously every day. "What? No, not me." Yes, you already actively spend time in meditation each day. Don't believe me? Well, let me ask you a question: "Do you worry?"

I don't know about you, but I'm very good at worrying.

I'm a natural. It's something I picked it up without anyone having to teach me. When I worry, I recall my problems and think about all the things that can go wrong.

But what is worry? Worry is meditating on the negative things in life. That's what is happening when we worry. We recall what someone said. Or we ponder our problems or some troubling circumstances. We chew on that idea in our minds and it fills our hearts with worry.

The good news is that if you are good at worrying, you can become good at meditation. All you have to do is to learn to focus on God's Word instead of the negative things of life.

THE HABIT OF MEDITATION

So how do you develop a heart for God? Simple. You begin by meditating on the Scriptures that God has already revealed to us.

In Jeremiah 29:13, God promises us that,

> *You will seek me and you will find me when you seek me with*
> *all your heart.*

God is not far away, but He is playing *hide-n-seek* with His children. When playing *hide-n-seek,* we all know that the whole purpose of hiding is that you want to be found by the seeker. God wants to be found by you. It's time for you to say to God, "Ready or not, here I come."

I believe that meditating on God's Word is among the most important habit that you can build in your life. I've made many mistakes along my spiritual journey, but this is one that I got right.

Since I was a young Christian, I developed the habit of consistently reading the Bible and keeping a journal of what God is teaching me. It's a habit that I have kept for years since I became a Christian as a teenager. God has used this one discipline as a tool to build my faith and shape my life more than any other.

So how do you get started? Well, I'm glad you asked. I know that Bible reading and meditation intimidates a lot of Christians. But it doesn't have to be hard or complex. You just have to get started and find your own rhythm. But if you don't know where to start, let me give you some practical suggestions.

1. Set a clear goal

If you want to build a new habit of meditation, you first have to answer two questions: What and Why?

- What is the goal of meditation?
- Why is meditation important?

The goal is not to learn more Bible knowledge or find

answers to theological questions. The goal isn't even to receive inspiration or encouragement from the Bible.

The goal of meditating on the Scriptures is to draw closer in your relationship with God. You want to grow in your devotion to God and get to know Him in a more intimate and personal way.

Here's a simple fact: the more time you spend meditating on God's Word, the better you will know God. And the more you know God, the more you will grow to love God. The goal of your meditation is not to study about God, but to spend time with God.

This is your WHY. This is your goal. The goal of this habit is to spend more time getting to know God more personally and intimately.

2. Choose a time and place

Researchers have found that we only accomplish 32% of the goals that we commit to. But there is one simple thing that you can do to double the likelihood of completing your goals. All you have to do is to find your WHEN and WHERE. Research says that if you select a specific time and place, your completion percentage increases to 71%.

It is important for you to choose the specific time and place you for your Bible reading and meditation. This one decision will more than double the likelihood that you will follow through with your goal.

So I encourage you to pick a consistent time when you

will spend time reading and meditating on God's Word. Be specific. Commit to a specific time. 7:30 AM is better than "sometime in the morning." Be consistent. This needs to be the same time each day. I know "life happens" and you will face interruptions, but try to be consistent.

I also encourage you to pick a specific place. Don't say, "at home." Where in your home? What room? Which chair? The more specific the better. The place you choose doesn't matter. It could be in your car, at the office, or in your home. Just be consistent. Have your Bible and journal ready. Make sure the place you choose doesn't have too many distractions. Just be consistent.

3. Follow a simple plan

Meditation and devotional practices are very personal and varied. Each person tends to connect with God in their own unique way. If you are getting started, I want to share with the simple plan that I use in my own devotions with God. This is what works for me.

Step 1 - Read a portion of Scripture

If you're new to Bible reading, or it's been awhile, I recommend that you start with reading the Psalms or the Gospel of Mark. Try to read at least a whole chapter. Read that chapter slowly, and more than once.

As you're reading, be aware of God calling your attention to a specific portion. Keep reading until a verse, phrase or thought jumps out at you. Once you have a specific portion you want to focus on, then you can move onto Step 2.

Step 2 - Record your insights in a journal

Once you have a Bible verse or phrase in your reading, rewrite that verse in a blank journal. In your own hand, copy the Scripture that you want to focus on. Rewriting the Scripture in your own hand will make a bigger impact than you think. This little action will help you focus on one idea that you will meditate on. This thought will stay with you throughout your day.

Step 3 - Write out your prayers to God

This is how I learned to pray. Early on, I felt self-conscious praying out loud, so I wrote down my prayers to God. If you are new to prayer, let me offer a pattern that you can follow. It's called the "ACTS" model of prayer. ACTS stands for Adoration, Confession, Trusting, and Seeking God's help.

Here are some prompts that can get your prayers started:

- Adoration: "God, I want to thank you for..."
- Confession: "God, I am sorry that I..."

- Trusting: "God, please help me to trust you with…"
- Seeking: "God, please show me what you want me to do today."

The "Seeking" section is not about talking, but more about listening to what God is saying to you. Ask God to speak directly to you and give you guidance. Listen carefully and record anything that God might be saying to you.

If you are new to doing your Bible reading or meditation, it may feel awkward at first. But please don't give up. The habit of Bible reading and meditation is essential to your spiritual growth. You cannot deepen your personal relationship with God without it.

SUMMARY

One of the key characteristics that made David *blessable* was that he had a *heart after God's own heart.* He pursued God. He spent time with God. He sought a personal relationship with God.

How do we develop that kind of heart? How do we develop the characteristics of *a heart for God?* Well, the best way to develop that characteristic is through the habit of meditation.

Meditation is not something that you have to stop everything else in life to do. Meditation is something that you do throughout the day. That's why it says, "meditates on your law day and night." You can think about God's promises on your commute to work. You can imagine and ponder God's character as you drive your kids to practice. You can even growl out a prayer to God as you wrestle with applying his word to your life.

Go ahead. Be like a cow. Ruminate. Trust me, you'll be blessed.

Chapter 4

HUMILITY

BLESSABLE CHARACTERISTIC #2

SAUL'S UNBLESSABLE PRIDE

In 1 Samuel 14, Israel is still at war with the Philistines. Saul is frustrated that the battle is taking so long. He believes that they should have beaten the Philistines much sooner. He grows impatient.

Israel's army has seen heavy battle. The troops are tired and discouraged. They are tired and hungry from fighting all day. They need a little break to rest and get some food before going back into battle.

But King Saul looks at his troops with disgust. He blames their lack of commitment for the battle taking so long. He attempts to fire up the troops and gives them a fiery half-time speech. This is where we see King Saul's pride at work.

This is what Saul says in verse 24:

Cursed is the man who eats food until it is evening and I am avenged on my enemies.

Here's my paraphrase of what Saul said:

What kind of lazy, terrible soldiers are you? Don't tell me you're hungry! Don't tell me you need to rest! If I see any of you men resting or eating before this battle is over, you're dead! I'm going to kill you myself, because it is my name and reputation that is at stake here!

I'm sure that motivated the troops. "Yeah, let's go out there and fight for Saul" was what the troops said NEVER.

Saul had a son named Jonathan. Jonathan was the best soldier and warrior in the whole army. He was the heroic figure that won the previous battle almost single-handedly. He was away when his father gave that command about not eating anything until the battle was over.

Later, Jonathan and the troops entered the forest. They found giant honeycombs with honey dripping down from trees. Jonathan took his spear and pierced a honeycomb and took some honey and ate it because he was hungry. It is said that Jonathan was refreshed and energized by the little afternoon snack. It was the biblical equivalent of drinking a can of Red Bull.

When the other soldiers saw Jonathan eating the honey, their mouths dropped open. They told him the king forbid them from eating anything until the battle was over. They said, "Your father said that he would kill anyone who ate anything before this battle is over."

When they went back to the battlefield, Israel kept on losing ground to the Philistines. This was because the soldiers were tired, hungry, and discouraged. But King Saul was angry that they were losing. He thought his soldiers were lazy and uncommitted.

Saul gathered the troops and said, "I know why we're losing this battle. Some of you have been eating today, haven't you?" Then he restated his oath to execute anyone who dared to defy his command by eating before the battle was over.

Saul was so angry that he got into this tirade. "Who has been eating today? I don't care who it is, I'm going to kill him. Even if it is my own son Jonathan, I'm going to kill him. Who was it?"

Then Jonathan answered, "It was me. I ate some honey." Now Saul's pride and anger has backed him in a corner. He just swore that he was going to kill anyone who ate, even his own son. To save face, Saul condemned his own son to death. But the whole army begged Saul to spare Jonathan because he was their battlefield leader. Saul finally relented and did not kill Jonathan.

This story is one about pride gone wild. This whole episode has nothing to do with fighting for God. It was all about Saul's personal pride. His motivation to win the battle that day was to avenge his name and his reputation.

So here's the takeaway: If you see a person who doesn't

care about anyone but themselves, do not follow that person. That person is a bad leader. They don't care about God. They don't care about you. They only care about advancing their own name. That is pure unblessable pride.

THE BLESSING OF HUMILITY

One characteristic that separates Saul and David is humility. Humility has never been a valued character trait. And that's still true today. Many see it as a form of weakness or insecurity. We tend to see boastful and prideful people as strong leaders, and humble people as weak.

But humility is not insecurity or low self-esteem. That is not a good understanding of the concept. Webster defines humility as "freedom from pride or arrogance." Humility is actually strength and personal confidence. It is having a realistic appraisal of yourself. It is knowing and accepting yourself as you are. Not allowing pride to over-inflate your own self-worth.

Self-centered pride leads to many negative character traits. Prideful people are always thinking of themselves. Often people who seem to have low self-esteem actually have issues with pride. Their pride makes them think too much of themselves. And when they don't measure up to the own expectations of themselves, it destroys their esteem. Often low self-esteem is pride in disguise.

Why do prideful people often look in the mirror and feel terrible about themselves? It is because the mirror doesn't match with the mental picture of how they see themselves in their own minds. They look at their bank statements and they feel terrible about themselves. That's because their current financial reality doesn't match with the lifestyle they believe they deserve. Pride and insecurity are closely connected.

DAVID'S EXAMPLE OF HUMILITY

David was a humble person from the beginning. Over and over God calls David, "my servant." That's even how David saw himself. David refers to himself as "the Lord's servant." Even after he becomes the King of Israel, he refers to himself as "the Lord's servant." Even to Saul, he calls himself "your servant."

Servanthood and humility was one of David's fundamental character traits. Where do we find David before he becomes the king? Serving others. He served his father as a shepherd. He served his brothers by bringing them food while they were soldiers. He even served the insecure and jealous King Saul.

God's hand of blessing and favor was on David for most of his life. But there was a season when God also removed His blessing from David as He did from Saul. This occurred when David stopped being humble and became prideful.

In 2 Samuel 11, we see a successful, middle-aged King David lounging around the royal palace. He is enjoying the fruit of his success. He was a Jewish version of Hugh Hefner in silk pajamas, slippers, smoking a pipe, and drinking mimosas in the morning.

Even though Israel was at war, David decided that he didn't need to go to battle this time.

He thought to himself,

>*I'm the king. I don't need to go and risk my life. That's why I have generals. I'll send them.*

David allowed pride to creep into his heart. He stopped seeing himself as a servant. He became prideful and started to take things that didn't belong to himself, including another man's wife.

David's pride led to the most regretful episode of his life: his infamous affair with Bathsheba, the attempted cover up and the murder of her husband Uriah. This tragedy was not birthed by lust, but by pride. David thought he deserved more. He pridefully thought he deserved to sit this war out. He pridefully believed he deserved Uriah's beautiful wife. He even pridefully believed he deserved God's continued blessings and favor.

As Proverbs 16:18 warns us,

>*Pride goes before destruction and a haughty spirit before a fall.*

STEALING SOMEONE'S THUNDER

You may have heard the idiom, "stealing someone's thunder." The background of that phrase comes from the days of William Shakespeare. There was a playwright by the name of John Drury who wrote a play that included the unique use of a brass bowl. This instrument made a realistic sound of thunder when struck. But that play was never produced. Instead the theater chose to produce *Macbeth* by Shakespeare. Shakespeare decided to incorporate the use of Drury's thunder machine into his play.

This upset Drury. He was angry at the theater and Shakespeare and exclaimed:

Damn them! They will not let my play run, but they steal my thunder!

The phrase, "stealing someone's thunder" is still used today. It means to take credit for something that is not yours. Or to do something to take the spotlight away from another person.

It may be rare to steal a thunder machine like Shakespeare did. But it is very common for us to "steal God's thunder" in our lives. We do this all the time. Every time we take credit for something that God does, we *steal His thunder*.

When God does a miracle, He wants credit for it. When He blesses a person, God is not only sending a message to the person being blessed. He is also putting His goodness on display for the entire world to see. But we often belittle God's role and attempt to take the spotlight away from God. We are not only "stealing His thunder," but we are stealing His glory. We have to be careful because the Bible says that "God will not share His glory with anyone" (Isaiah 42:8).

So, it makes complete sense that God is more willing to bless a humble person over a selfish, prideful person. The prideful person will try to steal a bit of glory for himself. They say, or at least think, "Oh, God has blessed me because I am so worthy of it! Come and honor me!"

But the humble person knows that they are completely undeserving of God's blessings. Therefore, they will readily give God all the credit that belongs to Him. Being humble makes you *blessable*. "God opposes the proud, but gives grace to the humble." (James 4:6)

THE ATTITUDE OF HUMILITY

So how do you develop the characteristic of humility? As you may have heard, humility is not "thinking less of yourself." Being humble is not having low self-esteem. Rather, humility is "thinking of yourself less." Pride comes when we are preoccupied with ourselves.

Philippians 2:3-4 gives us clear instructions about thinking about others before ourselves:

Do nothing out of selfish ambition or vain conceit, but in

humility consider others better than yourselves. Each of you
should look not only to your own interests but also to the
interests of others.

This Scripture is simple to understand but hard to do. It tells us to not do anything from our own selfish motives or for personal satisfaction. Rather, we are to think of others in higher regard than we think of ourselves. We are supposed to think about the needs and concerns of others before we think about our own.

These thoughts are clear. But how are we going to do this?

The passage of Scripture continues with some helpful insights,

Your attitude should be the same as that of Christ Jesus: Who,
being in very nature God, did not consider equality with God
something to be grasped, but made himself nothing, taking the
very nature of a servant, being made in human likeness. And
being found in appearance as a man, he humbled himself and
became obedient to death - even death on a cross! (Philippians
2:5-8)

This passage of Scripture tells us that there are at least two aspects of humility. First, humility is an attitude. Second, humility leads to humble actions. We talked about the attitude of thinking of others before we think about ourselves. Let's talk about the actions of humility.

HUMBLE ACTIONS

Verse 7 says that God humbled himself by taking upon himself the very nature of a servant. God took on flesh and became a servant in the man Jesus Christ. If you want to fight against the pride in your heart and grow the attitude of humility, a good place to start is to follow the example of Jesus.

Jesus said that He "came not to be served, but to serve" others. Our Lord is a servant and He provides for us an example to follow. The way we develop the character of humility is to build the habit of serving others. Serving others needs to become ingrained in our lives if we want to be people of humility.

One of the most beautiful pictures of Jesus serving others occurred on the night of the Last Supper. You can read the whole story in John 13. Jesus and His disciples gathered together in celebrate the feast of the Passover. During the meal, Jesus stands up and does the unthinkable. He strips down to His boxers and grabs a servant's towel and a basin of water. Then Jesus proceeds to wash each of His disciples' feet.

Getting your feet washed as you entered a home was an important part of the culture of that day. You can imagine how dirty their feet were. They walked around in sandals all day on unpaved, dusty roads.

Dinner was served on a low table or on the rug on the floor. You ate while sitting crisscross applesauce or reclining on your side propped up on your elbows. You couldn't hide your dirty feet under the table. Your dirty feet were open for all to see. I can't think of anything that would ruin my appetite faster than have someone's dirty feet in my face while I'm trying to eat.

At their Passover feast, there was no servant available to wash their feet. This job was reserved for the lowliest servant of the house. The Disciples waited around for the humble servant to take care of them. But there was no servant available to wash their feet that evening. So they went right on in and got down for dinner, dirty feet and all.

Jesus didn't wait for the servant to come and serve them. Jesus became the lowly servant. He humbled Himself and served each of His Disciples by washing their feet. He even washed the feet of Judas who would betray Him with a kiss later that night.

After washing their feet, Jesus taught His Disciples about serving others.

This dialog is found in John 13:12-17.

When he had finished washing their feet, he put on his clothes and returned to his place. "Do you understand what I have done for you?" he asked them.

"You call me 'Teacher' and 'Lord,' and rightly so, for that is what I am. Now that I, your Lord and Teacher, have washed your feet, you also should wash one another's feet. I have set you an example that you should do as I have done for you. I tell you the truth, no servant is greater than his master, nor is a messenger greater than the one who sent him. Now that you know these things, you will be blessed if you do them."

This story about Jesus washing feet teaches the attitude and the action of humility. It is a beautiful example of putting others first and serving them. Jesus was setting an example of what He expects His followers to do.

Jesus then reminds them that serving others is not beneath any of them. He reminds them that their Lord and Master is also a servant. If serving was not beneath Jesus, it shouldn't be beneath them either. Jesus wanted to teach them they are not too good or important to serve others. This is the key to humility.

You must see yourself as a follower of the *Greatest Servant of All*. In order to grow in humility, we need to destroy the root of pride in our hearts. To develop the character of humility, we must begin to make serving others a central habit in our lives. So where do we get started?

In our church we have a saying, "See a need and meet it. See a hurt and heal it." Look around you. There are needs all around. Get used to asking, "How can I help?"

In John 13:17, Jesus said,

Now that you know these things, you will be blessed if you do them.

If you make serving others a habit in your life, Jesus promises that you will be blessed.

So how do you develop the character of humility in your life? Well, like the answers to most Sunday School questions, the answer is Jesus. Do what Jesus did. Learn from His example and attitude. Emulate it. Put it into practice. Just do it.

THE HABIT OF SERVING OTHERS

Make serving others a way of life, where serving others becomes a natural part of your though process and routine.

If you want to develop the habit of serving, let me give you some suggestions to get you started.

1. Say "Yes"

The first step is to start to say "yes" to opportunities to assist people around you. When someone asks you to do them a favor, start to say "yes."

Can you give me a ride to the airport? Sure.

Can you help me move? Of course.

Can you lend me $200? Nope.

You can serve people, but you need to have boundaries or you will feel eventually used and become bitter. I have two general rules when I am presented with the opportunity to serve others.

Serving Rule #1: If I can, the answer is "yes."

I've already made the decision that the answer to every request for my help is "yes" if I am able. I try to be disciplined with my schedule and I know my priorities and limits.

I get asked to do a lot of things for people. I try to say "yes" as much as I can.

This allows me to not feel guilty when I must say "no" to requests for help that I cannot fulfill. I know my limits and boundaries. I jealously guard and protect my schedule and priorities. I make sure I'm taking care of myself, my family, and my responsibilities first.

Then when people ask me for help, and if I can help them, I always say "yes." However, sometimes a request is something that would interfere with one of my priorities. Then I will say "no" as politely as I can. And I do this without any guilt because I'm consistent with my rules.

I say, "I'm sorry, I wish I could help, but I can't right now."

Sometimes I tell the person the reason for my refusal. Sometimes I don't. Usually, the person doesn't feel bad because they know that I want to be helpful.

So do what you can to help others. Say "yes" as much as

you can. But you should know your limits. Do what you can, but don't try to do more.

Serving Rule #2: I am their servant, but they are not my master.

Jesus is the only boss I serve. Even though I serve others, they are not my master. I'm still in control of my decisions. I serve others because I choose to serve them.

I serve others because I love Jesus and want to follow His example. When I serve others, I am becoming more like Jesus. I don't serve out of obligation or guilt, but joy and love. I want to be helpful where I can. These two rules are helpful guidelines that protect me from doing too little and doing too much.

2. Ask, "How can I help?"

I've been a church planter for over a dozen years. My wife and I planted three churches and we never had our own building. We've held our church services in ten different locations. We met in schools, community centers, coffee houses, and even the haunted basement of a 100-year old church.

Each week, I would arrive hours early to set up the sound system and chairs for the worship service. My wife would set up the children's ministry space. When we first started, I did all the work. I even pulled a cargo trailer behind my under-powered 1996 Nissan Pathfinder. This cargo trailer contained everything the church owned. In those days, I was the Senior Pastor and the Senior Facilities Manager.

Soon after, God started sending people to help. A group of college students showed up and said the most beautiful words I have ever heard. Like when Forrest heard Jenny say, "You can sit here if you want."

These wonderful people asked me, "Pastor, how can we help?"

Those words brought tears to my eyes and confirmed the Sovereignty of God to my weary soul.

"How can we help?"

Hearing those words made me want to sing:

Ahhh, such beautiful, sweet words. As sweet as honey from the honeycomb! O how I wish I would hear these words from my teenage children. But alas!

If you want to develop a heart and a lifestyle of humility, start by asking someone, "How can I help?"

When those college students asked me how they could help, it was a turning point for our church. Instantly, I made them all interns and put them in charge of the set-up and a bunch of other things. I don't know how we would have made it through those early years without them.

Just try it. Go up to someone and ask, "How can I help?"

You will probably have to ask them more than once

because they won't believe that you're serious. They will probably say, "It's okay. I got it. I can handle it myself."

When you hear that, you must insist. "No, seriously. I want to help. It's no bother. Just tell me what you want me to do. Please let me help."

The underlying foundation of the "How can I help?" question is the lesson that Galatians 6:1 teaches:

Bear one another's burdens and in this way, you will fulfill the law of Christ.

What is the "Law of Christ"? We call that the Great Commandment. Jesus said that the whole law is summed up in a single statement. "Love God with all your heart, and love your neighbor as you love yourself." Helping is love in action.

There's a Hebrew proverb that says,

When God gives us burdens, He also gives us shoulders to help bear them.

Life's burdens are not for only one person to carry by themselves. Those burdens are supposed to be carried on the shoulders of the community. They are family burdens carried by the shoulders of the whole family of God.

So when we see others carrying heavy burdens, we

should help them carry those burdens. And when we do that, guess what happens? We fulfill Jesus' greatest desire for us. We are bringing glory to God by loving others as we love ourselves.

All that begins with the simple question: "How can I help?"

3. Check your motives

I used to run a food pantry at our church in Downtown Long Beach, California. Southern California has the largest homeless population in the nation. It's probably due to the temperate weather. I guess if you have to sleep outside, you would want to go someplace where it's warm and doesn't rain much.

Each week I would drive a box truck down to the Los Angeles County Food Bank to pick up food. My friend Ron and I would have to hustle and compete with the other charities to get the best quality food for our people. We were like Charles Barkley and Dennis Rodman boxing out for a rebound. Each week, we would hustle to find 15,000 lbs. of food to load up into our box truck to give to the needy folks in our neighborhood.

We took pride in being the best food pantry in our city. We had a group of consistent and faithful volunteers that loved serving others. There were lots of other places in our city where people could go and get food donations. But what set us apart was how we treated people.

It was our commitment to treat every person with dignity, honor, and respect. We never judged anyone. No yelling or disrespect. I worked hard to learn the names and stories of the regulars at our food pantry. I even picked up some Spanish so I could converse with the Spanish-speakers. I still refer to vegetables by their Spanish names. It's so much more fun to say *zanahoria* instead of carrot.

Every now and then, students from the local High School would show up to volunteer. We talked about our values of showing dignity, honor, and respect during our orientation. But these new volunteers were usually disinterested and bored.

We put these teens to work on the line. They distribute *zanahoria*, *repollo*, *pappas*, *cebollas*, and *elotes* to the needy folks in our community. But they would do it half-heartedly. They didn't smile or even look people in the eye. Sometimes we had to tell them to take their headphones off when serving others. Wearing headphones was a sign of disrespect.

Then after the day was done, these students would have time-sheets for me to sign. They were members of their school's community service club. They had to fulfill a certain amount of community service hours to be members of that club.

Here's a secret that I learned: High School students don't always volunteer at food pantries because they care about serving the needy. They volunteer because they want to be able to put it on their college applications. Most don't care about that homeless shelter or soup kitchen after they graduate. They are serving, but for selfish reasons.

Sometimes we also serve others for selfish reasons. We serve to distinguish ourselves, to get attention and earn praise. So check your motives for serving. Make sure you are not serving for your own selfish reasons.

Make sure you're serving, not to be seen or recognized, but to be helpful to others. Learn to find joy in the act of helping others. That's the reward. If you need to be seen or recognized for serving, that kind of serving will produce more pride in your heart. If you want to cultivate humility, you must learn to serve others with a good motivation. You should serve because you want to be helpful.

4. Do for one

Sometimes we don't serve and help people because the needs are so overwhelming. We think, "There are so many people in need. How could I ever make a difference?"

It's the lesson from that familiar parable about the boy trying to help the starfish get back into the water. As the story goes, a boy came upon a beach covered with starfish stranded on the sand. He started to throw the starfish back into the sea one by one. A passerby said, "Kid, don't bother. There's too many. You can't make a difference."

Undeterred, the boy picked up another starfish and threw it into the sea and said, "I made a difference to that one."

We've all been there before. The needs of people around us are overwhelming. We can't help everyone.

But just because we can't help everyone, does it mean we should do nothing at all? No, of course not. To see so many needs and do nothing is to be a part of the problem.

Pastor Andy Stanley has a saying that has guided me when I am overwhelmed by the needs of those around me. When we can't help everyone, we should still do what we can.

Andy Stanley says that we should,

Do for one, what you wish you could do for everyone.

We can't save every starfish, but we could save this one.

I can't mentor all these at-risk kids, but I can mentor this one.

I can't sponsor all these Compassion kids, but I can sponsor this one.

I can't fill all the volunteer needs at church, but I can fill this one.

Just do something. Doing nothing adds apathy and guilt to your soul. But at least doing something at least relieves one burden. It alleviates the problem a little. And it also allows you to feel good about your contribution however small it may be. You get to go to bed at night knowing that you've contributed.

SUMMARY

King Saul's pride made him *unblessable* to God. Instead, God choose to bless a young humble shepherd named David. David's humble attitude led to his humble actions of serving others.

Developing this character quality of humility will help shape you into someone who is *blessable*. And the best way to grow in humility is to make serving others a habit.

The goal of serving is to build up the perspective of Christ in our lives. When we serve others, we stop thinking about ourselves. And that's the beginning of true humility. Remember, humility is not thinking less of yourself, but thinking of yourself less and thinking of others first.

Find someone to serve today. Go up to them and ask, "How can I help?" Try it. You'll be blessed.

Chapter 5

INTEGRITY

BLESSABLE CHARACTERISTIC #3

THE HYPOCRISY OF SAUL

King Saul was a two-faced liar. He was a complete hypocrite. God gave Saul an assignment and he disobeyed. God wanted the Israelites to destroy a wicked tribe of Amalek. The Amalakites were evil people who kidnapped, raped, pillaged, and tortured their enemies. God wanted to send a message to the surrounding tribes that He took justice seriously.

God gave Israel the assignment to serve up justice to Amalek with the instruction that no one would be spared. They were to kill all the soldiers, the Amalekite King Agag, and all their livestock too. That seems pretty harsh. God wasn't playing any more games with Amalek.

In those days, the reason you went to war was to increase your wealth in land and resources. But God told Israel to kill everyone, and take nothing from Amalek. Take no spoils of war. Take no gold or silver. Don't make treaties with them. Don't even take their livestock. Kill everyone, including the animals and leave all their possessions behind.

God wanted to send the message that this battle was about divine judgment and not one motivated by the spoils of war. But King Saul only partially obeyed God's command. He did go to battle with Amalek and he did win a resounding victory in battle. He did kill all the soldiers, but he didn't follow through with the rest of God's instructions.

King Saul decided to spare the Amalekite King Agag. And as his men were about to kill the cattle and livestock of Amalek. Saul thought to himself, "Hmmm, this seems so wasteful to kill all these good animals. Let's save the best so we can have a BBQ!" So, Israel separated the choicest of the livestock, the best of the sheep and cattle, and took them home.

The Prophet Samuel confronted Saul about his failure to fully obey God's clear instructions. God told Saul to destroy the Amalakite army, King Agag, and all their animals and livestock.

When he saw the livestock, Samuel asked, "What are all these animals doing here? Why have you disobeyed God's command? Why did you spare these animals and bring them home?"

In front of the Prophet Samuel, Saul becomes became a meek little lamb. The Prophet Samuel was the only man that Saul feared because Samuel represented God. King Saul feared no one else.

Saul's answer reveal that he was a hypocrite at heart. He put on his mask and the performance was about to begin. "I feared the people and obeyed their voice," was his reply.

"I really didn't want to do it, but they made me," Saul tried to explain, "I was so scared of them."

Bravo! Encore! Encore!

What a great actor Saul was. He put on the mask of the frightened victim.

In reality, he was a tyrant. He feared no man. This is the same guy who tried to pin David to the wall with a spear in a fit of jealousy. The accounts of Saul's bravery and confidence in battle were legendary. But here, he put on a production for Samuel to try to excuse himself from his guilt. Of course, the Prophet Samuel saw right through this act. It would seem foolish to try to deceive to a prophet, wouldn't it?

INTEGRITY ON STAGE

The word "integrity" means wholeness or one. The cognates of that word are "integral" or "integer" meaning one or whole. Sometimes it is easier to define something by defining what is not.

What's the opposite of integrity? The opposite of integrity is hypocrisy. Being a *hypocrite* didn't always have the negative moral connotations as it does today. A *hypocrite* was what the ancient Greeks called an actor. Stage plays in Greece were either comedies or tragedies. The actors all wore masks on stage, either the *Guy Fawkes* happy face or sad face masks. They were playing a role, pretending to be someone they were not and pretending to feel emotions they did not. They were actors.

So, a hypocrite is someone who is playing a role. A person wearing a mask. He is acting. That character that you see on stage is not what the actor is really like. He is putting on a production or a performance for others to watch.

A person of integrity is the opposite of that. A person of integrity is not an actor. He does not wear a mask. His words and his emotions are his own. He is not putting on a performance for you or anyone else.

If you are a person of integrity, you are one person. You are the same person all the time. It doesn't matter the context or circumstance. Whether you're facing good times or bad. With rich people or poor. You do not wear masks. You are not trying to fake it. Your words and values match with your decisions and behavior.

A hypocrite is a different person in different circumstances. Saul was a hypocrite. He had several masks. Compare how Saul acted around his soldiers with how he acted around the Prophet Samuel. He was at least two different people.

DAVID'S EXAMPLE OF INTEGRITY

In contrast with Saul, David was a man of integrity. He was the same person in every situation. He was not perfect, but he had integrity. He was not a hypocrite.

You will clearly see this when you read David's Psalms. Most of the Psalms were written by David. They were his journal entries, his prayers, poems, and songs. The fact that David wrote out his deepest thoughts, doubts, fears and struggles for others to read show us that he has nothing to hide.

Was David perfect? Absolutely not. As successful as he was as a king, he was even more of a failure as a family man. His affair with Bathsheba destroyed his family. He had a good man murdered. His dysfunctional relationship with his son Absalom was heart-breaking.

But David never pretends he is perfect. He is quick to admit his fault. He openly acknowledges, grieves for, and confesses his sin. He tries to make restitution for all his mistakes. He owns them completely and publicly.

One of the first worship songs I learned as a new Christian was, *Create in Me a Clean Heart O God*. That song was inspired by Psalm 51. Psalm 51 is a heart-wrenching prayer of confession after the worst failure of his whole life.

I'm smiling because I remember singing that song in Youth Group, right before we began stuffing marshmallows into our mouths in a game called *Chubby Bunny*. David's soul was bared for all to see. Even for disinterested adolescents in youth group.

JESUS AND HYPOCRITES

If we want to be people that God can bless, we need to be people of integrity. God doesn't bless hypocrites. In fact, Jesus saved His harshest words for the hypocrites of His day.

The ultra-religious Pharisees were the biggest hypocrites of Jesus' day. When they came to hear Him teach, Jesus stopped the lesson He was teaching to confront them directly.

This is my paraphrase of Jesus putting these hypocrites on blast in Matthew 23:25-28

> *But woe to you, scribes and Pharisees, hypocrites! You only care about the outside, but not the inside. You only clean the outside of the cup, but the inside is still dirty.*
>
> *You are like whitewashed tombs, which outwardly appear beautiful, but within are full of dead people's bones. You appear outwardly religious to others, but inside you are full of hypocrisy. You brood of vipers! How are you going to escape God's wrath?*

I wish I could have seen their faces. If this was a YouTube video, it would have gone viral in two minutes. There would be comments like, "No HE DIDN'T!" and "OH

SNAP! Jesus just laid the SMACK DOWN!" That video would have had more hits than *Charlie bit me* and *Piano Cat* combined.

There is a reason that God hates hypocrisy so much. Hypocrites never deal with their sin or shortcomings. They are never contrite. Never poor in spirit. They only mask their sin.

Putting on masks is nothing new. It all goes back to the Garden of Eden. After Adam and Even sinned, they learned that they were naked and they became ashamed. So they sewed fig leaves together to cover up their nakedness. When God came around, they tried to hide from Him.

You may think it's silly to try to hide from God. But we do it every day. We still try to hide from God today but our fig leaves have become much more complex and sophisticated. We still wear masks today. We wear the masks of success, self-righteousness, religiousness, victimization, etc.

These masks are just sophisticated fig leaves we have sewn for ourselves so we don't have to deal with the fact that we sinned against God. We feel deep shame, so we try to cover ourselves.

If you want to be a person God can bless, take off your masks. Don't sew fig leaves for yourself. Fig leaves cannot cover your shame. But Jesus can. God covered Adam and Eve's nakedness with animal skins. God had to kill animals to make clothes for them. This is a foreshadowing of what Jesus does for us. Jesus was sacrificed on the Cross so that we can be clothed with His robes of righteousness. He covers our sin and shame. As the old song puts it, "Calvary covers it all, my past with its sin and shame".

To be covered and forgiven by Jesus, we need to be willing to take off our masks and admit our need for Him. We can't pretend with God. He knows our hearts. We need to stop pretending that we are okay. It is only when we admit we made a mess of our lives that we can turn to God to save us.

What's even more harmful is that hypocrisy has a side-effect of preventing us from being truly loved. To be truly loved, we must first be truly known. If we have our masks of hypocrisy on, we can never be known.

So, let's live mask-free lives of integrity. Let's be like David. Yes, he failed, but he didn't try to cover it up. He was open with his failure. He grieved for his mistakes, asked for forgiveness, and sought to make amends for his sin. That is a picture of integrity. No wonder God blessed him.

My youth pastor friend asks his students this question, "Are you the same person in church as you are on Facebook or Snapchat?"

That gets to the heart of integrity. Are you one person in all places? Or do you put on masks and play the actor in different environments? If you do, then you are a hypocrite. Sorry. Sometimes the truth hurts.

TAKING OFF OUR MASKS

So how do we develop the characteristic of integrity in our lives? Since hypocrisy is about putting on a mask and playing a role, we need a place where we can take off our masks. We tend to wear an assortment of masks. We tend to play multiple roles for others to see. We wear the masks of perfection, politeness, spirituality, and success. But behind the mask we are never as put together and confident as we want others to believe.

We need to be a part of a community of people that will love and accept us as we are. We need a place where we can be fully authentic and fully known and accepted. The Bible calls this "fellowship." Fellowship has lost much of its meaning today. It has been called, "Two fellows in the same ship." And don't look at me, bail!

Many of our churches have a "Fellowship Hour." This is where churchgoers drink coffee and chat after the church service. Many churches have an old dusty room in their basement that they call the "Fellowship Hall." This is where the potluck suppers are eaten.

But fellowship is so much more than small talk and potlucks. It is the sharing of life together with a group of people. It is doing life with people who you consider to be like a "friend that sticks closer than a brother" (Proverbs 18:24).

We need these people in our lives more than we like to admit. We need the people that we can begin to be authentic with. If we are to become people of integrity, we need true fellowship. We need to have people that can help us shed our masks with their love and acceptance. Finding a community like this is not easy, and for many it is the most difficult and rare thing imaginable.

I have been a part of a small group fellowship of some kind since I became a Christian as a teenager. Sunday School Class, Small Group Bible Study, Discipleship Group, Men's Group, etc. I cannot recall a prolonged season when I was not involved in a small fellowship group. I've gone through seasons of ups and downs in my faith. I've had seasons in which I didn't read the Bible or pray or serve.

But there was never a season in which I didn't show up in community with other believers. My wife and I have hosted Small Group Bible Studies in our home for years. Fellowship and community have been among God's greatest tools to help grow my faith. Without being in fellowship with other believers, I could have never taken off my masks.

I grew up in a broken family and went through some painful experiences of rejection as a child. Because of that, I had a tough time letting people in. So I became very good at wearing masks. It was being a part of a loving and accepting fellowship that helped me take the risk of being vulnerable and shedding my protective mask.

It was only when I learned to take off my masks that I found deep security in the love and acceptance of God. It is my hope that we all could experience the amazing healing power of fellowship and community.

THE REQUIREMENTS OF COMMUNITY

This is where it gets practical. Let me show you the secret to becoming a person with integrity. You need to develop the habit of fellowship and community. The Bible encourages us to be a part of a community of people that you can invest in and that will invest in you.

Hebrews 10:24-25 says,

> *And let us consider how we may spur one another on toward love and good deeds. Let us not give up meeting together, as some are in the habit of doing, but let us encourage one another - and all the more as you see the Day approaching.*

There are a few insights that we can learn from that passage of Scripture about the habit of community. Here are the four requirements of community:

1. Fellowship requires a common goal.

You cannot have true fellowship with others unless you all have the same goal. The common goal is to help each other move "towards love and good deeds." Our community is not bound together by our common interests or political views. It is our common commitment to help each other grow that unites God's people in fellowship.

We come together with the commitment of helping

each other grow in faith and devotion to God. This is evidenced by our commitment to meet together. We are intentional in the way we help each other grow as we encourage each other and "spur one another on toward love and good deeds." This common goal of helping each other grow in our faith is a necessity in the formation of true fellowship.

2. Fellowship requires vulnerability.

Author Brene Brown says that vulnerability is key to emotional and relational health.

She writes:

> *Vulnerability is the birthplace of love, belonging, joy, courage, empathy, and creativity. It is the source of hope, empathy, accountability, and authenticity. If we want greater clarity in our purpose or deeper and more meaningful spiritual lives, vulnerability is the path.*

Being vulnerable is not easy. It takes a lot of courage to take our masks off and let others see us as we truly are, warts and all. It takes courage because there is the possibility of rejection.

But never taking our masks off ensures that we will never enjoy any true intimacy. Not with God, others, or even ourselves. The masks we hide behind feel like a comforting and protective shield. But in reality, our masks become a prison that trap us with fear.

We fear that if we take off our mask for others to truly see us, they may think less of us or even reject us altogether. That's why being a part of a community of people where you can take off your masks requires so much courage. Brene Brown says, "Courage starts with showing up and letting ourselves be seen."

3. Fellowship requires intentionality.

Verse 24 says that we should "consider how we may spur one another on towards love and good deeds." Verse 25 says that we should "encourage one another." This Scripture is filled with active verbs that requires intentional effort. It takes effort, thought, commitment, and intentionality.

We should sit down and "consider" ways that we can help each other grow in our faith. We have to try to "spur one another on." We have to think about how to "encourage one another." None of these actions will occur without intentionality. This is why true fellowship is so rare these days.

4. Fellowship requires consistency.

Verse 25 encourages us to "not give up meeting together, as some are in the habit of doing." We all want to experience true fellowship with people and enjoy authentic community. This environment is not built overnight. It requires consistency. To paraphrase G.I. Joe, "Showing up is half the battle."

This is where fellowship and community needs to become a habit, a way of life. Do not give up meeting together. Sometimes the most important thing you can do is show up. We know that fellowship and community is more than showing up, but it is not less than that. It starts with showing up.

If you want to grow in your integrity, find people that you can be vulnerable around. Invest in a group of people that will help you take off your masks. That's the best thing you can do.

FIVE COMMITMENTS OF COMMUNITY

Community doesn't just happen. True fellowship doesn't grow on trees. I'm talking about the *Fellowship of the Rings* type of fellowship. Not the coffee and donuts after church kind.

So, let's get practical. Let me suggest five things you can do to begin to develop the habit of community with leads to a life of integrity. Here are five commitments you need to make if you want to develop a healthy community.

Commitment #1 - Show up consistently

You need to find a group of people where you can be yourself. Where you can let yourself be known by others. Where you can start to build a foundation of trust. This will help you begin to feel comfortable enough to begin to remove your masks.

Being vulnerable is difficult. It's not wise to be vulnerable to everyone all the time. That's a quick way to get hurt. But you need to have at least a small group of people to be vulnerable with.

This is the amazing beauty and value of the local church. Churches shouldn't be only places of learning and inspiration. Churches should mostly be places of community. I cannot stress enough how important this is. Regular involvement in a community of faith is essential to your character and faith development.

We are living in strange times for the church. There's been a dramatic shift about how people participate and attend a local church. The scandals and politics of "institutionalized religion" frustrate and disillusion many Christians. So they decide they no longer need to attend any church. They may keep their faith in Jesus, but they lose their church membership.

Or many Christians abandon their small churches and choose to be a part of an anonymous mega-church crowd. They don't want to invest in relationships. They don't want people to really know them. They like their masks. This is a problem.

Okay, I'm not bashing big churches. This is what I'm saying you need to do. Go to church. Get in a small group. This is especially important if you attend a large church. You can't know everyone. You can't be known by everyone. But you need to know and be known by some.

If you want to grow, you need to find a consistent small group of people that you commit to doing life with. And I'm not talking about just your family. Because if you only have your family, who are you to go to for support when you're having difficulty in your marriage?

Sociologists say we have the relational capacity to maintain only eight to fifteen close relationships at any one time. So, you need to be intentional about finding your eight to fifteen. Once you do, show up consistently.

Go to that small group meeting even when you had a rough day at work, or just argued with your spouse. Just show up. It's good for you and your presence is good for them.

I know that church attendance is not mandatory for your salvation. God loves those with poor church attendance just as much as the ones that earn gold stars in Sunday School. I understand that involvement in a small group of believers is not mandatory for salvation. But it's essential for your faith development.

Anne Lamott is one of my favorite authors. She writes about her love for her small church family:

> *The main reason is that most of the people I know who are doing well psychologically, who seem conscious, who do not drive me crazy with their endlessly unhappy dramas, the only people I know who feel safe, who have what I want - connection, gratitude, joy - are people in community. And this funky little church. It is where I was taken when I had nothing to give, and it has become in the truest, deepest sense, my home. My home-base.*

As with most Christian parents, she forced her son to attend church as a child against his protests.

She writes:

> *And there are worse things for kids than to have to spend time with people who love God. Teenagers who do not go to church are adored by God, but they don't get to meet some of the people who love God back. And learning to love back is the hardest part of being alive.*

Anne is right. You can find God anywhere. You can listen to the world's best preachers on your iPhone. You can sing along with the livestream of megachurch worship services. You're just as loved by God if you stay home in your jammies as if you go to church.

But when you don't show up, you're missing the most important part. You're missing out on being in relationship with other people who are trying their best to love God back. You can't get that off the internet. You need to show up if you want that.

Commitment #2 - Listen with Love

When you show up consistently, bring your whole self there. My mentor says that the most valuable thing you can bring to any community is your "transformed and transforming presence."

Your presence has power to transform any environment. And your presence is most powerfully felt when you listen to others with love. Empathy and compassion are so rare in our culture today. People make snap judgments and form opinions about others so quickly. And a lot of the time, the judgments and opinions are negative.

A community of people who listen to each other with love and empathy is rare. But it is one of most life-changing experiences you can have. This is the secret magic of 12-Step Recovery groups. They listen to each other.

Listening is a super-power that has the ability to transform both the one talking and the one listening. Learn to show up consistently and listen with love. Don't show up just to talk or to learn. Listen with love and empathy. It will change your life.

Something strange happens when we learn how to

listen to others with love. Listening helps develop our heart's capacity for empathy and compassion. Our heart goes out to others when they are honest and vulnerable about their challenges and struggles.

Through listening, our Grinch-sized heart grows four sizes. Listening to others has a special side benefit for us. It helps us gain the courage to be honest and vulnerable ourselves. Then we can begin to show compassion to the person that we are hardest on: *ourselves.*

We judge and criticize ourselves so easily. Listening to others helps us learn to listen with empathy to ourselves. Showing compassion to others helps us give ourselves permission to show ourselves compassion too.

Listen to others. Listen to God. Listen with love. Listen to your own heart. Listening has transformational power.

Commitment #3 - Affirm Others Intentionally

Words of Affirmation is my primary love language. For many people it is. We must deal with so many negative messages aimed at us throughout our day.

We get negative messages from all directions. The media makes us feel inadequate. Not enough. Not beautiful enough. Not thin enough. Not successful enough. Not enough.

This is what the whole multi-billion dollar marketing industry is based on. The sole purpose of marketing and advertisement is to make us feel like we are not "enough."

That there is something missing in our lives. And the only way we can feel "enough" is to buy whatever miracle product they're selling.

We also get negative messages on social media. I'm not referring to the mean trolls and their overt Haterade. I'm talking about the pictures and announcements your friends post about their amazing new boyfriend or girlfriend. Their dinner at that 5-star restaurant. Their fancy vacation. Their new expensive purchase. Or pictures of their kid doing something remarkable.

Your friends don't mean to intentionally make you feel bad (well, maybe some do). But they unintentionally force you to compare your life with theirs. And somehow you always feel like your life doesn't measure up with theirs.

Let me set the record straight here. What people post on Facebook, Instagram, Twitter, or Snapchat is not real life. Social media posts are not accurate representations of a person's life. Your friends don't go on vacations every week. They don't go on fancy dates every night. Their kids aren't that amazing and they don't win awards every semester (well, some do, but we don't like them very much).

It's a foolish thing to compare what you know about your life with the highlights of someone's best day. If you measure yourself against those curated, Instagram-filtered, and Photoshopped posts, you can't win.

There's no way you will feel good about yourself. It's a negative message you don't need. And it's not real. It's as real as a *reality show* on TV that somehow makes the

Kardashians seem as happy and normal as *The Brady Brunch*. It's fake propaganda that you shouldn't compare yourself with.

It's hard to live in this world with all these negative messages flying at us. And the most hurtful negative messages are the ones we tell ourselves. No one is immune to negative self-talk. Life beats us all down. We all have bad days.

Do you know what gives life to discouraged people? Do you know what will quench the thirstiest soul?

A simple word of affirmation. A well-placed word of affirmation can build someone up like nothing else. I was 40 years old before I heard my Mom say, "I love you." Old school Asian immigrants just do verbalize their emotions well. Even though I never doubted her love for me, I cried like a baby when I finally heard her verbalize it. I can't tell you how much my soul needed to hear her express her love in words.

If you want to build someone up, use words. Well-placed words of affirmation are among the most powerful tools for building community.

As you give words of affirmation to others, something strange and amazing happens. You'll begin to allow yourself to receive and believe others when they affirm you. Which brings us to our next commitment.

Commitment #4 - Receive from others

Showing up to give and affirm others is easy compared to this commitment. When you show up to give to others, you are still in control. You remain in the power position in the relationship.

It takes humility to receive from others. But community cannot be one-directional. You must learn how to receive from others.

When someone gives you a word of affirmation, you must learn how to receive it with humility and grace. It's so easy to mask our pride with false humility. Only prideful people have difficulty receiving from others.

This was my problem (probably still is). I couldn't receive anything from others. I didn't want to owe anyone anything. I wanted to be self-sufficient and independent. I didn't want to be so weak that I needed something from anyone. Within the context of community, I showed up to give and help others. But out of pride, I could never receive.

When someone gave me a compliment or word of affirmation, I would reject their gift. I would do it subtly and politely, but I would not receive it. Thanks, but no thanks. I don't need it.

I would say things like:

- Don't mention it.
- It was nothing.

- It was no effort at all.
- It was no big deal.

What a jerk! Since then, I've learned that it was a defense mechanism. My inability to receive from others was a way to keep people at arm's length. Subconsciously, I believed that if I received their affirmation that I would begin to rely on it. And when I needed more affirmation, they would let me down.

Learning to receive was difficult for me. Now I'm truly thankful when people offer their help or affirmation. Instead of brushing helpful people away, I've learned to pull them closer. I've learned to graciously receive their words. Now I respond by saying, "Thank you for saying that. That means a lot to me."

Another interesting side-effect occurred when I learned to receive encouragement from others. I began to be more open to receiving words of affirmation from myself. I stop saying negative words to myself. I've learned to encourage myself and receive it graciously.

That's how community and trust is built. Give and take. Trust, compassion, and reciprocation.

So next time someone does or says something nice to you, just say, "Thank you. I really appreciate that. That means a lot to me."

Imagine if you were a part of a whole community of people like that. Trust me, learning to receive from others will go a long way toward creating the community of fellowship.

Commitment #5 - Ask for help

Here's the final commitment that will help you develop the habit of community. Learn to ask for help.

Asking for help requires humility and vulnerability. You must admit that there's a part of your life that you can't do by yourself. That's hard because you have to be honest about your shortcomings.

Asking for help is the advanced version of the previous commitment of learning to receive from others. Whereas the previous commitment was passive, this one is active.

"Receiving from others" is responding well when others try to help you. But "asking for help" is taking the initiative to seek help. It's admitting you need help and trusting others will not reject your request. It takes a lot of humility and trust to ask others for help.

It's amazing how quickly trust is built when you ask someone for their help. It's one of the fastest way to build relational trust. When you come into a relationship only to give, you remain in the power position in the relationship. But when you ask someone for help, you are intentionally placing them in the power position.

You are saying to them, "I trust you enough to admit I need your help." Not only will this help you gain the help you need, it will also help you gain a lot of friends.

SUMMARY

Integrity is such a rare and valued commodity in our world today. Integrity is best build within the context of a community. We all need a safe place to take off our masks.

Integrity isn't about being perfect. It's about being honest and open with your imperfections. The best way to prevent hypocrisy from creeping into your soul is by developing the habit of community.

You need to be a part of a group of people that will allow you to be honest and vulnerable, a family of people that will love you and accept you, warts and all. A community where you can let yourself be truly known and loved.

Hypocrites are created by fake, insincere community that encourages the wearing of masks. People of integrity are found in authentic and vulnerable communities.

Go and find one. Or create one yourself. Then be fully present with those other people who doing their best trying to love God back. Trust me. You'll be blessed if you do.

Chapter 6

FAITHFULNESS

BLESSABLE CHARACTERISTIC #4

THE UNFAITHFULNESS OF SAUL

K ing Saul is a fitting example of an unfaithful person. He was not someone you could depend on. His loyalty changed with the wind. One day he loves and praises David, and the next he tries to kill David out of jealousy. One day he praises God, and the next he openly disobeys God.

Saul had everything going for him. He was more gifted and talented than anyone else in Israel. He was the best-looking, tallest, and strongest around. He was from a wealthy and respected family. He had the position, respect, and authority to do so much good. But he squandered it all on himself. Somehow, he thought God's blessing was for him to consume and enjoy for himself.

Out of pride and selfishness, Saul wasted God's blessings and opportunities. Because he was unfaithful with it,

God had to remove His hand of blessing and protection from Saul and redirected those blessings to young David.

BLESSABLE FAITHFULNESS

When I think of the idea of faithfulness, I picture an old married couple who stayed together for 50 years. Now that's a picture of a faithfulness.

I think about my father-in-law Steve. He is a model of faithfulness to me. He has loved his bride well for over 45 years. He's the husband of one wife, never having eyes for any other woman. But Steve's faithfulness wasn't just that he never committed adultery. It's how he loved his wife each day since he said, "I do."

He was faithful with his presence and attention. He was faithful in putting bread on the table. He was faithful in the raising of children together. He was faithful with her in all the doctor's visits and hospital stays. Now, in retirement from over 40 years of ministry, he is even a faithful volunteer at my church.

What is faithfulness? Some say that being faithful is simply showing up when you're supposed to. I think there's a little more to it than that. Faithfulness is more than just showing up. But it is not less than that. Faithfulness begins with your presence.

Faithfulness is not situational, but a foundational part of your character. God likes to bless people with the character quality of faithfulness. Being faithful makes you *blessable*.

In Matthew 25, Jesus says:

If you are faithful with little, I'll make you master of much. But if you are not faithful with the small things, even that I'll take away from you.

God is a wise manager of His resources. Why would waste His blessings on an unfaithful person? Instead, he seeks to bless a person who has been shown to be faithful with a responsibility.

In my church planting ministry, one of the things that I get to do is assess potential pastors to see if they would make good church planters. I love doing this, and I'm pretty good at it. I can usually tell within a few minutes of asking questions if the candidate would do well in this role. I don't ask questions about passion or philosophy. I ask questions about the pattern of their past behavior.

The questions go something like this: "So tell me about a time when you did _____." You can fill in that blank with whatever you are looking for.

- So, tell me about a time when you started something new.
- So, tell me about a time when you raised money and recruited people.
- So, tell me about a time when you lead someone to Christ and discipled them to maturity.

The best indicator of one's future performance is past behavior. If they can't show me that they were already faithful in the past, that's not a good sign. It makes me doubt that they are ready to be trusted with such an important task.

God does the same thing in the distribution of His blessings.

DAVID'S EXAMPLE OF FAITHFULNESS

David is a notable example of faithfulness. We know he wasn't perfect. He had some terrible and public failures. Despite his failure, he was faithful to return to his responsibilities after repentance. David's story encourages me because it shows that a person can fail and still be faithful.

You can see David developing this pattern of faithfulness from an early age. When we first meet David in the Bible, he is a young pip-squeak runt. He was the youngest in his family and he knew his role and responsibilities.

His father Jesse gave David the job of taking care of the sheep. A shepherd was considered one of the lowliest jobs in that day. It was the job you took when you couldn't find any other work. No one wanted to be the shepherd, so they made the youngest do the dirty work. I know what it feels like to be the runt in the family. I have four older brothers and it wasn't always fun.

His brothers didn't want the job of shepherd, so they made

David do it. David showed up and was faithful to his shepherding responsibilities. One of his responsibilities was to protect his flock of sheep from attack from wild animals. It was during this time that he taught himself how to throw rocks with a sling with deadly accuracy. He learned to use the sling so that he could be a good shepherd and protect his sheep.

When the predators attacked his flock, David didn't run away. He was faithful with his assignment. He risked his life to fend off predators, killing a lion and a bear as they tried to eat his sheep. We know that God used David's unique skill with the sling later when he dueled Goliath. But he gained that skill while being faithful at a task that no one else wanted. No one was paying any attention to him, no one but God.

David was also a faithful servant to others in authority. He was taught to respect those in authority over him. He respected and obeyed his father. He served his older brothers by bringing them food when they went off to battle. Respect for authority was drilled into him from an early age. This helped him be faithful to King Saul even when Saul went bonkers and tried to pin David to the wall with a spear.

David was also faithful with a special talent God gave him. He was a musician and poet. What was said about Alexander Hamilton could be said of David, "his skill with the quill is undeniable." He didn't let that skill go to waste even in dark times. He faithfully wrote down songs, poems, and prayers. He wrote during good days and bad. Today we call many of his writings, *The Psalms of David*.

WHAT ABOUT YOU?

David was faithful with the gifts, resources and assignments God gave him. What about you? Are you faithful with what God has given you?

God has entrusted each of us with so many things in life. We need to be faithful with what God has given us. We have to remember that God doesn't bless us so we can consume and enjoy it all for ourselves. These blessings are to be used for God's purposes.

Once, I heard an African-American preacher give a powerful sermon on faithfulness. I can still hear his powerful voice in my head. He alliterated his points and delivered it in the cadence only Black preachers can.

He said that God has given each of us these four things that we must be faithful with.

1. Treasure
2. Talent
3. Time
4. Testimony (pronounced: "Tes-ta-mo-NAAY!")

Treasure refers to money and resources. Talent refers to skills and natural abilities like preaching and singing. Time is obvious. Testimony refers to experiences, wisdom, and life lessons.

That's what God has given each of us. How are you using it? Are you being faithful with what God has entrusted to you? Or are you just wasting it on yourself?

God has blessed us with many resources. Knowledge, position, experiences, influence, relationships, opportunities, abilities and many other things. We need to learn to be faithful with what God gives us.

We have three choices of what to do with God's blessings. We can consume them for ourselves. We can waste them. Or we can faithfully invest these gifts for God's purposes. We get to decide what to do with God's blessings.

Great blessings require great faithfulness. But the problem is that most people do not even realize how truly blessed they are. They don't think they're truly blessed because they don't have much *treasure* in the bank, or *talent* they can put on display for others to see. They think this excuses them from the responsibility of faithfulness.

People think, "I'm just a normal person. I don't have much to give to the world." That's not true. Even if you don't have a lot of *treasure* or *talent*, you're still richly blessed with *time* and *testimony*. In my opinion, *time* and *testimony* are far more rare and valuable than *treasure* and *talent*.

There are wealthy and gifted people all around us that make zero impact for God. I can honestly say that I have been much more impacted by someone investing their time and testimony in my life than anything else.

Maybe you're not gifted. You're afraid of public speaking. You can't sing or teach. Or you don't have much money to give. What you don't have doesn't matter. You just have to be faithful with what you do have.

You're not responsible for what you don't have. What matters is if you are faithfully using what you do have for God. No matter who you are, you have *time* and *testimony*. Start there. Be faithful with that.

CAN GOD TRUST YOU?

One of the most inspirational stories about faithfulness is the story of Rick Warren. Rick is pastor of Saddleback Church, which is about 20 minutes from where I live. He is most known for writing *The Purpose Driven Life*. That book is the best-selling hardback book of all time. It's now the most widely printed, translated, and distributed book of all time, second to only the Bible itself.

Overnight, Rick received amazing publicity, wealth, and recognition. He has appeared on Oprah, Larry King, CNN and many other media outlets. He's been featured on countless magazines covers and in news stories.

His fame spread even wider when there was a news story of a woman who was abducted by a kidnapper at gun point. With the SWAT team outside the door, she read to her abductor passages from *The Purpose Driven Life*.

Rick's words touched the kidnapper so deeply, he repented, and asked for forgiveness. He released the woman and went outside and turned himself in. The story of how this book saved this woman's life and changed her kidnapper made headline news. There is even a movie about this amazing story.

I was invited to Saddleback Church with other pastors in the community to spend time with Pastor Rick. What Pastor Rick told us that day changed the way I see and seek blessing from God.

Rick told us that he knows that God has blessed him in a great way. He acknowledges that the success and influence of that book was all God's favor. It was not anything he could have accomplished for himself. He gave all the credit to God.

This is what Pastor Rick told us,

Do you know why God blessed me?

I know exactly why He blessed me. God knew that He could trust me with that blessing because I have been faithful with what He has already given me.

Then Pastor Rick went on to describe his lifelong journey of faithfulness to God. He told us that, since he got married, he and his wife decided to increase their financial giving to God each year. They started giving 10%, then 11%, then 12%.

Every year, they gave more and more back to God's work. Their generosity kept on increasing. They were up to

20%, then 30% and then 40%. They gave back to God more and more.

Pastor Rick stated that his goal was to give away 90% of his income and live on only 10%. He called it *Reverse Tithing.*

When Rick's book became a runaway best-seller, he became a multi-millionaire overnight. Tens of millions of dollars came his way.

Do you what Pastor Rick did? Did he go out and buy new cars and a mansion? Did he buy a private jet?

Nope, he chose to drive the same Toyota pick-up truck he always did. His family continued to live in the same home they raised their kids in.

Pastor Rick calculated how much Saddleback Church paid him for all his years as their pastor. Then he wrote a check to repay every penny they paid him.

He started a foundation that champions his "Global PEACE Plan." The goal is to plant new churches, provide medical care, education and assist people in underdeveloped nations.

Then, with the biggest grin you can imagine, Pastor Rick told us:

> *Kay and I have become Reversed Tithers! We give God 90%, and we live off 10%. And next year, we are going to give away 91%!*

Why has God blessed Pastor Rick so greatly? God is a

smart manager of His resources. Because Rick was faithful with all the little blessings over the years, God saw fit to bless him with much.

Is faithfulness something that a person can develop? Or is it an innate quality that only some people have?

Well, I hope it is the first option because I would be hopeless otherwise. I don't naturally have faithfulness. It is true that the Bible says that we are born into sin with wicked and deceptive hearts. And, it is only through the mighty work of God that we are redeemed and restored and given a new beginning. Yet, as with every character quality, faithfulness is not innate. We do not have it, but it is something that we can receive from God and develop.

JESUS BLESSES FAITHFULNESS

One of the most famous stories that Jesus told was the *Parable of the Talents* (a talent was a unit of measure for gold that equaled about 20 years' wages for a laborer). This story is also called the *Parable of the Bags of Gold*. If you want to read it, you can find it in Matthew 25. This parable teaches a clear lesson about faithfulness. Jesus highlights the lesson by rewarding the faithfulness and punishing unfaithfulness.

To the faithful, the master said,

> *Well done, good and faithful servant. You have been faithful over a little; I will set you over much.*

He said of the unfaithful servant,

You wicked and lazy servant! Take the talent from him and give it to him who has the ten talents.

The servants were each given great sums amounts of money, some more than others. But with that great blessing came the great responsibility to invest it wisely.

If you are a fan of superhero movies, you are probably familiar with the reoccurring moral lesson of the *Spider-Man* movies. In it Uncle Ben tells Peter Parker, "With great power comes great responsibility." And no, I don't think Jesus stole that idea from reading comic books as a kid. I would bet that Stan Lee went to Sunday School and heard that parable told on a flannelgraph board.

Luke 12:48 says,

Jesus said, "Everyone to whom much was given, of him much will be required."

Rachel Cruze is Dave Ramsey's adult daughter. Dave is the guru behind the *Financial Peace University*. Rachel tells a story of how her father taught her siblings and her how to be responsible and faithful.

He used the metaphor of a rope. The rope represented their freedom. If they wanted more rope, they had to show that they could make responsible decisions. If they were faithful, they would get more rope. If they were not faithful, he would pull the rope back in and they would have less freedom.

Eventually, they would learn to be faithful and responsible. He would no longer have to hold onto their rope. Then they would be adults who are responsible for their own lives and decisions. Before they went off to college, Dave held a *Rope Ceremony* for each child. At the ceremony, he would give the child a rope to symbolize that they have shown themselves to be faithful and responsible enough to take full control of their lives as adults.

Wise parents know the way to teach their children to become faithful and responsible. It's not a mystery. If you want responsible kids, you have to entrust your child with a little more responsibility a little at a time. And this is exactly what God does with us.

He wants to bless us, but we have to show that we can be faithful with His blessing. Too much blessing given to an unfaithful servant becomes a curse. Don't believe me? Look at what happened to the Prodigal Son when he got his share of the inheritance. Look at all the horror stories of the ruined lives of lottery winners.

So, faithfulness is learning to be responsible for what we have already been given. The concepts of faithfulness and responsibility are closely connected. One cannot be faithful unless they take full responsibility. A faithful person does not cast blame or make excuses. They take 100% responsibility over their actions. So, faithfulness begins with the mental shift in ownership and responsibility.

Faithfulness is a muscle. It grows when you start small and work on it day after day. People are not born faithful. People do not become faithful overnight. Faithfulness is built, grown and nurtured over time through repeated behavior.

THE PERSPECTIVE OF STEWARDSHIP

So how do I grow to become a more faithful person? Great question. I'm glad you asked. If you want to become a more faithful person, the best place to start is to develop the perspective of stewardship. A steward is a person who manages the finances or property of another person. It's like when a wealthy person creates a trust fund and makes someone else the executor of their wealth.

The steward plays a key role in managing the wealth and riches of the estate. But the estate does not actually belong to the steward.

Fellow *Lord of the Rings* nerds know Boromir could never be King of Gondor, because his father was only a Steward of Gondor. Their family was only keeping the throne warm for the true heir of King Elendil.

Faithfulness begins with seeing ourselves as stewards, or managers of God's blessings, and not the final recipient or owners of these blessings. Today, stewardship has primarily come to refer to how much money we give to the church.

Usually, this occurs in the forms of tithes and offerings. This sells the concept of stewardship short.

Yes, we are to be faithful managers of God's money. And yes, we should faithfully give to our local church. But money is only one of the resources that God has entrusted to us to manage for Him. He has given us many other blessings besides money. We have knowledge, position, influence, relationships, time, passion, etc.

We need to be faithful stewards of those resources alongside the financial resources. How do you invest your *talents*? Maybe you can mentor some kids. How do you invest your *time*? Your presence has the power to transform another person's life. How do you invest your *testimony*? God has brought you through some hard times and taught you some valuable lessons. Don't keep these blessings to yourself. Don't bury them in the sand. Be faithful. Invest these blessings for the benefit of someone else.

However, I believe the clearest expression of faithful stewardship is how we handle our money. Financial stewardship is the most fundamental form that faithful stewardship will take. If a person is not faithful in how they manage their money, they will not be faithful in the other areas of life either.

This is one example of how our attitudes about finances reveal our heart. As Jesus said, "Where you treasure is, there your heart will be also."

WHO ARE YOU ROBBING?

Personally, I don't like to talk about money. But the Bible talks about it a lot, so I can't get away from it. The Bible says that when we don't give back to God a portion of what He's given to us, that we are "robbing God."

Malachi 3:8-9 says,

> *Will man rob God? Yet you are robbing me. But you say, 'How have we robbed you?' In your tithes and contributions. You are cursed with a curse, for you are robbing me, the whole nation of you.*

Ouch. That's a bit harsh. Those are some direct words. This passage of Scripture is revealing why, perhaps, you haven't been experiencing the abundant flow of God's blessings in your life. Heaven's windows of blessing have been shut for you because you haven't been faithful with the blessings God has already given you.

Malachi says when we don't give to God, we are "robbing God." But that's not the only person we're robbing. We're also robbing ourselves.

Malachi 3:10 says,

> *Bring the full tithe into the storehouse, that there may be food in my house. And thereby put me to the test, says the Lord of*

hosts, if I will not open the windows of heaven for you and pour down for you a blessing until there is no more need.

God is more than willing to bless us. All we have to do is show that we are *blessable* by being faithful with what He's already given us.

This is a painful lesson that I had to learn over and over because I'm not very smart. Coming from a poor immigrant family, scarcity and frugality was a way of life. I didn't grow up with the security blanket of wealth.

For most of my life, I thought money was the answer to all my problems. That it was the source of security, significance, and happiness. I couldn't shake this mindset even when I became a Christian. Even though I trusted God with my soul, I couldn't trust Him with my money. I faithfully served God and the church. I volunteered in youth ministry and even became a pastor. I faithfully invested my *talent*, *time*, and *testimony*. But I couldn't give Him my *treasure*.

I'm embarrassed to admit this, but I didn't start tithing consistently until after I got married. And that's only because my godly wife made me. Learning to tithe and give generously to the church and to ministries and missionaries around the world was a huge breakthrough for me. When I did this, God kept His end of the bargain. He opened up the floodgates of heaven and started pouring out His blessings on me and my family.

I'm not referring only to financial blessings, but blessings in all forms. Yes, God has sent financial blessings our way. God has richly provided for us every material thing that we need. We're not rich. We live in a rented house. And I'm still paying off student loans. But I'm blessed with more than I need and more than I deserve.

Learning to tithe also had an amazing and unexpected side-benefit. Somehow, giving money away did something in my heart and my soul. It helped to break the false emotionally dysfunctional connection I had with money. I was trapped in a poverty and scarcity mentality where I saw money as my source of security and the solver of all my problems. I thought the only way I could feel safe, secure, and significant was to have more money. So I hoarded it. I served money. Money became my master.

Now I know what Jesus meant when He said, "You can have only one master. You cannot serve both God and money." I was serving money. Money was my master. And the only way I was released from this prison was by learning to be faithful in giving money away.

I'm not saying I don't have issues with money anymore. Money will probably continue to tempt me to find my identity and security in it. But through giving, I'm no longer bound and trapped in a life dedicated to serve the god of mammon (Matthew 6:24). I now know that money is a false god, a lifeless idol. Money promises security and significance. But it can never deliver on those promises. Only God can.

Now I've learned, and continue to learn, to be faithful to return and invest all of God's blessings back to Him. I want to be faithful with giving back to God because I know that He is the true source of my security and significance. I'm loved, accepted, secure, and safe in Him. He gives me significance. I'm His child. I'm loved by God. What's more secure and significant than that?

THE HABIT OF GIVING

I would encourage you to begin the habit of regular, consistent and proportional giving back to God to your local church. If this is new for you, let me offer you some suggestions.

1. Acknowledge: "This is not mine"

The first step is to acknowledge that what you have doesn't belong to you. You are only a steward; a manager. It's not your money. It's God's money. Everything that you own are gifts that have been given to you by your loving Heavenly Father. God has provided you with everything. Your beating heart, the air in your lungs, and even your ability to work and earn a wage. All that comes from God.

Acknowledge God's ownership over you and your stuff. It's more freeing this way. As Corrie Ten Boom said, "Hold everything in your hands lightly, otherwise it hurts when God pries your fingers open."

2. Take 100% responsibility

No more blaming or making excuses of why you are not being faithful. The reason you are faithful or unfaithful has everything to do with you. It is no one else's fault. Take full responsibility.

3. Start Small and be consistent

There's a debate whether tithing (the giving of 10% of your gross income) should be taught as a requirement of discipleship. I think that whole debate is a bit misguided. The goal of the Christian life is to give all of yourself to God as a living sacrifice. So it's not really about whether or not you give 10%. It's really about who you're living for. However, if you're not giving at least 10% of your finances back to God, there's no way you are living 100% for God.

If you're not giving regularly, you have to start somewhere. You may not have much, but you can start where you are. I recommend starting with giving a percent or two, or whatever you are comfortable with. Don't worry about the amount at first. Just focus on the mindset and the consistency. Commit to give proportionally, a specific percentage not a specific amount, with the goal of getting to at least 10%. If God blesses you with more, you can do what Rick Warren did and try to give a higher percentage next time.

Here's a tip that has been helpful for me. Sometimes I

don't give because I just forget. So now I automate my giving. If your church has a way for you to give electronically, I recommend automating your giving. Just set it as a reoccurring payment each month. Even if your church doesn't have an electronic giving set-up, you can do it yourself by contacting your bank and setting up an auto-payment.

4. Prayerfully invest

If you follow the steps above, you will find that your mindset will begin to change. You will begin to see that there are many other things that you need to be faithful with. Perhaps, God will ask you to give more of your finances to bless others. Or He will ask you to be more faithful with your time, or your talents. Go to God in prayer and ask, "Lord, how do you want me to invest the resources you have given me?"

SUMMARY

We all want to be blessed by God. One of the characteristics God is looking for in the people to bless is the characteristic of faithfulness. Faithfulness makes you *blessable*. When we're faithful with the small blessings, God sees that He can trust us with the bigger blessings.

We need to learn to be faithful with all of God's blessings. God blesses all of us with *treasure, talent, time,* and *testi-*

mony. We have to learn to be good stewards of all these resources.

An essential way to become a faithful person is to develop the habit of financial giving. Developing this habit isn't easy, but it will grow your character. If you never learn to be faithful to God in your finances, you will never be faithful with the other parts of your life either.

So, if you want to develop and grow the character of faithfulness in your life, where should you get started? If you haven't yet, you should develop the habit of financial giving. Start with developing a habit of the faithful and proportionate giving of your finances back to God through your local church. You'll be blessed if you do.

Chapter 7

PATIENCE

BLESSABLE CHARACTERISTIC #5

THE IMPATIENCE OF SAUL

The Israelites were preparing for battle with their nemesis the Philistines. The Prophet Samuel sent word to King Saul to tell him to wait until he arrives before going into battle. Samuel was scheduled to arrive in 7 days. When he arrived, he would offer a special sacrifice to ask God for His blessing and protection in battle.

Samuel sent a message to Saul that was absolutely clear,

> *Do not go into battle without me. I will arrive in seven days to offer a sacrifice to God and ask for His blessing.*

King Saul was not a man of patience, and did not wait for Samuel.

1 Samuel 13:8-11 says:

He waited seven days, the time appointed by Samuel. But Samuel did not come to Gilgal, and the people were scattering from him. So Saul said, "Bring the burnt offering here to me, and the peace offerings." And he offered the burnt offering. As soon as he had finished offering the burnt offering, behold, Samuel came. And Saul went out to meet him and greet him.

Samuel said, "What have you done?" And Saul said, "When I saw that the people were scattering from me, and that you did not come within the days appointed, and that the Philistines had mustered at Michmash...

On the morning of the seventh day, the Prophet Samuel was nowhere to be found. Saul's troops were getting anxious. Across the battlefield, they saw the Philistine army assembling and preparing for battle.

King Saul decided to do something absolutely forbidden in the Bible. He took it upon himself to offer God a sacrifice before the battle. Only prophets and priests were given the honor of offering sacrifices to God. Saul was not a prophet or priest, but a king and a warrior. A person who has "blood on his hands" was forbidden to offer the sacrifice. Saul knew that this was forbidden, but he couldn't wait any longer. He was impatient.

That sounds like the beginning of almost every regrettable mistake I ever made. "I couldn't wait any longer. I was impatient."

Have you said those words yourself? You were impatient and made purchases that you couldn't afford, so now you are in debt. You were impatient and you couldn't wait for God to bring the *Mr./Ms. Right* into your life, so you settled for *Mr./Ms. Right Now,* and at this point, you regret that decision. You were impatient and couldn't wait on God to resolve a problem, so you took it into your own hands and made the situation worse.

As we will see, a little patience goes a long way.

Verse 10 says,

> As soon as [Saul] had finished offering the burnt offering, behold Samuel came...

If only King Saul would have waited an hour longer. Samuel was not actually late. He told Saul that he would be there in seven days. He didn't say when on the seventh day he would arrive, but just wait for him. Saul assumed that because Samuel was not present at sunrise on the seventh day, he would not be coming.

This little moment of impatience cost Saul his kingdom.

In verses 13-14, Samuel told Saul:

> You have done foolishly. You have not kept the command of the Lord your God, with which he commanded you. For then the

Lord would have established your kingdom over Israel forever.
But now your kingdom shall not continue.

The Lord has sought out a man after his own heart, and
the Lord has commanded him to be prince over his people,
because you have not kept what the Lord commanded you.

This was a seemingly small mistake brought on by Saul's impatience. But this mistake led to Saul's removal as the King of Israel. Saul disobeyed the direct command of God. If Saul had obeyed, God would have established Saul's right to rule Israel. But because he disobeyed, God would take the Kingdom away from Saul and give it to another person.

EVERYONE HATES WAITING

I am not a patient person. I hate waiting. I don't know a single person who enjoys waiting. I wait in lines at the store, the bank, and in rush hour traffic. One of the places that I find myself waiting a lot is at restaurants.

It seems like all the good restaurants make you wait a long time. You have to wait to get a table. You have to wait to get your drinks. You have to wait for them to take your order. You have to wait for them to bring your food. You have to wait for them to bring your bill. That's a lot of waiting.

And the thing that gets me is that they have the audacity to call THAT guy "the waiter"! What? Really? He's not the waiter. I'm the waiter here! I've been waiting all night long!

My wife tells me that I'm an impatient person. As with most things, she's right. I struggle with impatience so much. And it's not just with people, it's also with God. I often ask, "How long, O Lord, am I supposed to wait?"

But I have come to realize when I question God's timing I am actually questioning God himself.

When I question God and become impatient, this is what I'm saying to God:

God, my plan is better than your plan. My way is better than your way. I am wiser than you are. You are late. You're timing is off. I'm not sure if I can trust you.

So, if you see impatience as a constant pattern in your life, this may be a sign of something seriously wrong in your soul. Impatience is not a small thing. Impatience isn't just having nervous energy. It is a symptom that reveals a deeper problem. Impatience reveals a lack of trust and confidence in God's ability, timing or wisdom.

When you are impatient, you are doubting the wisdom and the goodness of God.

Being impatient is saying to God:

God, I'm not sure what you're up to, but I don't think you're doing a good enough job. Because if I was in charge, it would have been done by now. I'm going to take it from here. So why don't you move over and just let me do my thing.

We make excuses for our impatience. We say, "I'm just not a very patient person." If you have said that, what you are saying is that you are not a person that trusts God very much. You don't trust that God will bring about His perfect plan in His own perfect timing.

THE BIGGEST TEST OF FAITH

I am learning that often the most difficult form of faith is waiting. For me, the most difficult form of faith isn't charging up the hill into battle. It's not jumping out of the boat and walking the on water. The hardest form of faith is waiting.

While you are waiting, God usually doesn't show you what He is up to behind the scenes. Waiting on God takes 100% of our faith, because we don't see anything happening.

This is the essence of faith itself. Hebrews 11:1 says that faith is having "confidence in what we hope for and assurance about what we do not see." Faith is believing in something that you do not see. You don't see God at work behind the scenes preparing the pathway for you. You don't see God removing the obstacles in the way. But even though you do not see God at work, you choose to believe in Him and you wait on Him and His timing. That is faith.

Impatience isn't merely minor character flaw. Impatience is faithlessness. Impatience reveals your lack of faith and confidence in God Himself. Impatience reveals you don't believe that God is who He says He is or that He's going to do what He said He would do.

DAVID'S EXAMPLE OF PATIENCE

While Saul was impatient, David was good at waiting. David patiently waited for God's plan to come to pass. He did not take it upon himself to "grab his moment."

Patience was one of David's best qualities. David was anointed to be the next King of Israel by the Prophet Samuel when he was still a teenager. He was an unknown. He was a young kid that no one expected anything from.

When Samuel showed up at his father Jesse's house to find the next King of Israel, they ignored David. Jesse didn't even bother to invite young, pimple-faced David to the selection party. But David was the one that was chosen by God to replace Saul.

The Prophet Samuel laid his hands on David and pronounced him to be the next king. But the problem that Saul was still king and David was still going through puberty. This was before David killed Goliath, so it is easy to see why David was patient. He knew he wasn't ready.

But David's patience would get tested many times. After David killed the giant Goliath and became a famous warrior, he was still patient. He waited for his time. He didn't take it into his own hands. Even when Saul became jealous of David and tried to kill him, David remained patient.

David had two separate opportunities to kill Saul and take his rightful place as the new king, but he didn't. When Saul and his army went looking for David in the desert, King Saul needed to make a pit stop and take a potty break. Saul entered a cave to relieve himself. He didn't know that just around the corner in that cave hid David and his band of mercenaries.

David's men encouraged him to take matters into his own hands.

They said,

David, this is your time. This is your opportunity. You can become the King today!

God has delivered Saul into your hands. He is in his most vulnerable state. Why don't you kill him so we can stop running?

But David didn't take matters into his own hand. He didn't want to take the throne by force. He wanted to wait on God's perfect timing. He spared Saul that day. This did not happen only once, but it happened on two separate occasions. There was a second time when Saul came close enough for David to kill, but David was patient. He trusted God's timing. God rewards us when we wait on Him and His timing. When you are impatient it shows a lack of trust in God's wisdom and character.

HOW LONG, O LORD?

Patience is one of the more difficult qualities to develop. This is especially true if you believe that God actually has a plan for your life. Many saints throughout the centuries can relate to David's repeated prayer: "How long, O Lord?"

Have you ever prayed these prayers to God?

- How long, O Lord, before you remove my obstacles?
- How long, O Lord, until you open these doors for me?
- How long, O Lord must I endure my present situation?
- How long, O Lord until I see your hand of favor in my life?

I've prayed similar prayers far more times than I can count. You probably have too. But be encouraged. Though those prayers seem like prayers of doubt, they're not. They are actually prayers of faith.

These prayers are from a person who is going directly to God with their problems. They are not taking matters into their own hands, but crying out to God for help. When you pray similar prayers, you're not trying to take control of the situation on your own.

You didn't say,

God, where are you? Okay, forget it. If you're not going to do it for me, I'll do it by myself. Thank you very much!

David prayed those prayers during his many dark nights of the soul. He prayed those prayers in a cave, as he hid from Saul's men who were hunting him down. Those are prayers of dependence and faith.

Don't be embarrassed that you have prayed those prayers too. God wants to hear us wrestling with Him. Patience and waiting have a way of forcing us to be dependent on Him.

During those times of waiting, all we have to hold onto is our confidence in the character and promises of God.

Pastor Andy Stanley defined faith this way:

Faith is having confidence that God is who He said He is and that He'll doing everything He said He would do.

Praying "How long, O Lord?" isn't showing a lack of faith in God. That prayer actually reveals that you believe God is going to come through on His promises. And you are eagerly anticipating God coming though. It's the giddy expectation my kids have for Christmas morning. "Daddy, how long until we can open the presents?"

One of the reasons we have a difficulty with waiting is because we see it as wasted and unproductive time. We think, "I could have gotten so much done by now." But we need to see that waiting is one of God's primary tools of preparation.

Waiting is so productive for our soul. Waiting time isn't wasted time. Waiting accomplishes more than you know. Waiting is one of the most effective and formative experiences for the development of our character.

THE VALUE OF WAITING

You may have heard about the famous "marshmallow test." It was a research study done by the evil sociologists at Stanford University in the 60s and 70s. They tested 32 young children on their ability to "delay gratification." Delayed gratification is the fancy, grad school phrase for "waiting."

They put the kids in a room, one at a time, tempted by a fluffy and delectable marshmallow placed tantalizingly in front of them. They told each kid that they could eat the marshmallow or wait and they would get two. The researchers then left the room and watched how the kids reacted from behind a one-way mirror.

Predictably, some of the kids didn't wait and ate the marshmallow right away. Others struggled for a few long seconds or minutes. Most succumbing to the powerful draw of the Stay Puffed Marshmallow Man before their time was up. A few succeeded in waiting the entire duration. These were rewarded with a second marshmallow.

The insightful part of this research was the follow up process. The researchers followed these kids into adulthood. They wanted to see if there was a connection between the ability to delay gratification with success. They later interviewed these kids as adults, ten years and then 20 years after the original experiment.

The research is telling. Compared to the impatient kids, the children with the greater ability to wait, became far more successful as adults. They had higher college entrance test scores, got better jobs, and accomplished more than the impatient kids.

The Stanford study shows that waiting is a great and necessary skill to have to be a productive human being. If you are a parent, imagine if you never taught your children that they had to learn to be patient.

What kind of child would you raise? I'm not saying that impatient children will all become axe murderers. But I probably wouldn't invite your rude and impatient kids over for a play-date with my kids. Just saying. Good parents teach their children how to learn to wait and be patient. God is a good parent, too. He is teaching us the same thing.

What does patience accomplish? That's a good question. Waiting is very humbling. I hate to wait. And that is because I'm prideful. I live in Southern California with twenty million other prideful people. There are long lines for everything. I have to wait at the grocery story, the bank, the post office, and the airport. And don't get me started about waiting in lines at Disneyland! They should call that place Disney lines. I even have to wait to use the bathroom in my own house!

Waiting is humbling. Because, even though I think I'm a super-special snowflake, I'm reminded that I am human just like everyone else in this line. I am not more important than anyone else. I can't cut in front of them. I'm not more special than they are. I don't deserve special treatment.

If someone cut to the front of the line at the grocery store, people would get angry and shout, "Who do you think you are? Get in the back of the line like everyone else!" Waiting has a way of reminding you that you are human.

Waiting also has a way of focusing your attention. When you're in line at a bank or grocery store, you are focused on the clerk at the front. Maybe he is having trouble. Maybe they will open up a new line.

When we wait on God, we are focused on Him. We are not trying to figure out our own solution to the problem. When we cry out, "How long, O Lord?" our attention is fixed on God. It is not doubting God, but showing confidence that He will intervene, you just don't know when. When you finally receive the blessing or answer to prayer that you've been waiting for, you are more apt to acknowledge that this blessing came from God. This is because you were focused on Him.

Waiting also prepares you to properly receive the blessing God wants to give you. Timing is everything. When you have to wait for something, you are more thankful for it when it finally comes. You treasure it more. If you waited a long time for it, the blessing isn't likely to be something that you would take for granted. You've agonized and sweated out those prayers. Now you're even more thankful.

One of the things I've learned as a parent is that it is good to teach my kids to wait. My son wanted a new Alienware gaming computer. That was the *Red Ryder BB Gun* on his wishlist. He's a good kid and I wanted to get it for him. But I said, "Yes, but not yet."

We set up a list of things he would have to do and how long it would take for him to get that computer. He wasn't getting that computer if he did poorly in school or disrespected our house rules. He would have to earn a portion of the price of the computer himself by saving up his allowance and doing extra chores. He would have to wait. When he finally got that computer, he was much more thankful and has been taking care of it well.

God has taught me a lot about waiting. It is funny how I have a different perspective on waiting. Waiting is terrible while you're going through it, but waiting is actually not bad when you look at it in the rear-view mirror.

God does a lot of internal soul work in my life while I'm waiting for Him. While I'm waiting for His blessing, He is at work in my heart. Waiting seems to be the only time that

I'm still before God. It's the only time that He has my full attention.

When I look back on the *wandering in the wilderness* times of waiting on God's hand of favor, I do so now with gratitude. I learned that I was totally unprepared to received God's blessings at the time that I first asked for them. If God would have blessed me too soon, I would have been a terrible manager of those blessings. It would have ruined my life. And I would have wasted those opportunities. I would be like those millionaire lottery winners who go bankrupt within a few years.

I'm smart enough to know it wouldn't be a good thing for God to give me everything I want when I want it. I would become the most prideful, immature, ungrateful and self-indulgent person you can imagine. Too much "blessing" given to a person who is not prepared for it is not a blessing at all, but a curse. You can see how celebrities struggle with fame and wealth. They can't handle it. So they make foolish decisions that hurt themselves and those close to them.

Water is good at the right time and place. But too much water at the wrong time and place can be a devastating flood that destroys lives. Fire is good at the right time and place. But fire at the wrong time and place can burn your house down. The same can be said about God's blessings in our lives. God knows if, how much, and when we can handle His blessing. That's why we need to be patient and learn to wait on His timing.

THE PERSPECTIVE OF WAITING

So how do you develop the character quality of patience? I think patience comes from having perspective. It's knowing what is really important, and what is not. You could be tempted to lose your patience with your kids when they make noise and disturb your nap. But when you remember what you really value is not silence, but having a loving family, it helps you not to lose your temper. That's perspective.

Patience comes from perspective. And perspective helps us be patient. So where does perspective come from? For me, the best place I know to gain perspective is through keeping a prayer journal. I have been writing my prayers down in a journal for almost three decades. I have dozens and dozens of journals all around my home and office.

These journals have given me perspective on what God is doing in my life. Somewhere in my garage is a box of old journals from when I was a brand-new Christian. Like David, I cried out, "How long, O Lord?" Sadly most of my prayers back then where not about deliverance from enemies, but about my sad dating life. Yes, my deepest most heartfelt prayers were about my teenage feelings towards some girl in youth group who spurned my best efforts.

These old journals are precious to me. Every once in a while, I pull one out and read it for kicks. As I go back and read these journals, two things happen. First, I remember what a shallow loser I was. (This, by the way, also helps with building characteristic #2 of humility.) Second, these journals give me perspective.

I am reminded that God has always been faithful to me. He was always present in my ups and downs. He was there with me when I walked through those valleys of the shadow of death. These journals act as my own personal *Footprints in the Sand* bookmark. Through my journals, Jesus reminds me, "When you saw only one set of footprints, it was then that I carried you."

THE HABIT OF JOURNALING

If you want to become a more patient person, the best advice that I can give you is to start journaling. If you are new to journaling, let me give you some suggestions.

1. Just start small and make it a habit.

Get a cheap paper journal from the dollar store and just start writing. Don't buy those expensive Moleskines for your journals. Even though Moleskines may earn you some hipster street-cred at the coffee shop, they are a waste of money. Because they cost $15, you subconsciously don't want to waste its precious pages on your "unworthy" thoughts. Don't do that. Just buy a cheap composition notebook or dollar store journal.

Don't worry about what you write in your journal. It doesn't have to be formal. I keep a journal with me everywhere I go and I write in it every day. I write out my thoughts, grocery list, list of people I'm praying for, insights from my personal study of the Bible, and a bunch of other random thoughts. But mostly I write letters to God and even to myself (I'll explain this in the next section). But the key is to just get started and be consistent.

2. Write out your prayers.

I write letters to God. I write out my prayers in letter form. I usually start a new page and write "Dear Lord," at the top and just write out my prayers as if I would be speaking them out loud. This helps me get past my ADHD mental roadblocks.

I would also suggest taking some time to listen to God and write down what you believe God is saying to you. We know that prayer is two-way communication. So, if I gain some insight from my Bible reading or prayers, I write those down too. Usually, I write down something like: "God, I hear that you are telling me _____. Is that what you are saying?"

It's my way of recording my "insights from God" to refer to later. Most of the time, these "insights" are terrible, ill-formed, and illogical thoughts. They probably didn't come from God at all. But sometimes I find a golden nugget hidden in there. It was the process of writing it down that helped me receive and discern what God is trying to tell me. However rare, God has spoken very clearly to me many times through this process of journaling.

3. Write letters to yourself.

I also write letters to an imaginary version of myself that I call "Mr. Morning Pages." I adapted this idea from a book by Julia Cameron. I write in the pages of my journal every morning, so hence the name. I write a letter to Mr. Morning Pages and I complain to him about all the things that I have to do that day. He is a good listener. This process helps me focus and gives me an outlet to complain.

It is also helpful because I like to separate how I talk to God and how I talk to myself. I've found that when I write to God, my language is more formal and calculated. But when I write to Mr. Morning Pages, I can be more casual and authentic.

4. Re-read your past journals.

This is where you will gain your perspective. You will see that the things that you were so worried about a month or a year ago, were not life-ending problems at all.

You made it through. It wasn't nearly as bad as you thought at the time. And God came through. He didn't abandon you but showed you that you could trust His faithfulness. You will be able to trace God's faithful presence throughout your life. This will help you to be patient in your current situation because you know that the same God who never let you down before is present with you right now.

SUMMARY

Patience is the greatest test of faith that I know of. Waiting is hard, but it has a purpose. I remember struggling through my own prayers of "how long, O Lord?" But now I'm so thankful that God made me wait. If He would have answered my prayers early on, it would have ruined my life.

Earlier in my life, I was completely unable to manage and steward His blessings well. I was too immature and unaware of my own shortcomings. I was like a 16-year-old who asks for his own car. Some can handle the responsibility that comes with that blessing. Some cannot.

What will make waiting easier is perspective. Perspective allows us to be patient. And the best way I know how to gain perspective is through the habit of journaling.

We need to learn to trust in our Father's timing and methods. Trust Him. He is good and wise. He is never early, but always right on time. Be patient. It makes you more *blessable.*

Chapter 8

REPENTANCE

BLESSABLE CHARACTERISTIC #6

SAUL'S LACK OF REPENTANCE

Being a good person doesn't mean that you are always going to get it right. We're all going to make mistakes along the way. Mistakes and failure are a necessary part of life. Dave Ramsey calls it paying your "dumb tax."

Failure and mistakes are the most powerful teachers and mentors that can help you learn and grow. That is, if you are willing to admit your mistakes and learn from them. But too often, when prideful people make mistakes and fail, they don't like to admit it. They either try to cover it up, blame others, or make excuses, or all of the above. This is what we see King Saul doing.

After the episode we discussed earlier about King Saul failing to destroy the Amalekite livestock, the Prophet Samuel confronts him about his disobedience. When he saw the Prophet Samuel, King Saul happily greeted him.

Here's my paraphrase of what Saul said to Samuel:

Blessed be you of the Lord. I have performed the commandment of the Lord. We kicked their butts and won a resounding victory! I completed the assignment that God asked me to do.

Then Samuel confronts Saul and said,

Saul, if you did what God wanted you to do, then why do I hear the bleating of sheep and the lowing of oxen? What are all these animals doing here? You were not supposed to take any of the spoils of war!

At this point, Saul was caught red-handed. He made a terrible mistake. Even though he won the victory, he failed the mission. This mission was supposed to be a message about God's divine judgment upon the evil Amalekites. But now it will seem like it was just another battle fought for financial gain.

What does Saul do? Does he admit his mistakes and failure? Will he learn from them and vow never to repeat this mistake? That is what any good leader would do, and that is exactly what Saul does not do. Instead, Saul tries to cover up his failure and make excuses.

Sadly, we continue see this pattern in our politicians and leaders today. It is rare to see any of them admit to making a mistake, ask for forgiveness, and vow to learn from it.

Instead they do a combination of three things: 1) cover it up, 2) justify it, and 3) blame others. And this is exactly what King Saul does.

It would have been so easy for Saul to admit his failure when Samuel confronted him. He could have said, "You're right. I didn't follow God's command. I failed. Please forgive me. I promise to never do this again." But Saul didn't do that.

HOW NOT TO REPENT

We can learn a lot from Saul about exactly what NOT to do when we fail or make a mistake. Here's four things that Saul did that we should try to avoid at all costs.

1. Cover up your mistakes.

Saul did not admit his mistakes, but rather he tried to explain them away.

This is what he said to Samuel:

> *I have obeyed the voice of the Lord. I have gone on the mission on which the Lord sent me. I have brought Agag the king of Amalek, and I have devoted the Amalekites to destruction. (1 Samuel 15:20)*

Did you notice that Saul doesn't admit to his failure? He

says, "I have obeyed the voice of the Lord." You could imagine how frustrating it was for Samuel to hear this.

This is reminiscent of the impeachment hearings of former President Bill Clinton. In 1998 in which he was asked if he is having sexual relations with Ms. Lewinsky. He categorically said "no". Then later he was asked by a grand jury if he perjured himself by lying under oath. He famously answered, "It depends what the meaning of 'is' is."

Saul did the same grammatical gymnastic routine in trying to explain away his failure to obey God. He said, "I have obeyed the Lord. I won the battle. We destroyed their army. I did obey God." But Samuel saw right through this, and pressed him. In my mind, this is how the conversation between the two went:

Saul: *"It's done. I completed the mission. We won the battle. I have obeyed the Lord's command."*

Samuel: *"Really? How much of the Lord's command did you obey?"*

Saul: *"Well, most of it. I did the big and important stuff. We won the battle. I completed the mission."*

Samuel: *"Well, why did you spare King Agag? And what about all these animals? Why did you spare them? That was part of God's commands too."*

Saul: *"Okay, you're right. I did take home some of their best sheep and cattle. But I did obey God's command and completed the assignment."*

Samuel: *"You're not answering my question. How much of the Lord's command did you obey?"*

Saul: *"Most of it. At least 80% of it. I think 80% is pretty good. Don't you?"*

Saul never admits to his failure. He only highlights what he did right, and ignores his mistakes. Any half-intelligent person will see right through this. You would lose respect for the person who never owns up to his/her mistakes.

It is better to come clean and admit your failures up front. It shows that you are aware of your actions and you are sincere in wanting to learn from that experience.

2. Justify your mistakes.

Once Samuel nailed him to the wall, Saul had to admit his failure to fully obey God's command. But then Saul switches tactics and tries to justify his actions. Saul justifies his actions by coming up with an excuse. He said the reason he spared the livestock was to "sacrifice to the Lord your God."

Saul tries to justify that the reason that he disobeyed God was actually a good reason. He claimed that he only wanted to honor God by sacrificing these animals as a burnt offering.

But Samuel saw right through this excuse too.

He corrected Saul by saying:

Has the Lord as great delight in burnt offerings and sacrifices, as in obeying the voice of the Lord? Behold, to obey is better than sacrifice, and to listen than the fat of rams. (1 Samuel 15:22)

To paraphrase Samuel, he told Saul,

Stop trying to justify your failure. Stop pretending that you were trying to do something good for God. If you really wanted to honor God, you should have just obeyed him. Don't you know that God cares more about your obedience than anything else?

Far too many of our people continue to follow the example of Saul. Instead of admitting our mistakes and learning from them, they justify and explain why it was a noble thing that they were trying to do.

3. Blame others for your mistakes.

Probably the most common tactic of not admitting our mistakes is blaming others. Saul does this very well. Saul shifts the blame on his men for the failure to destroy the livestock.

In verse 1 Samuel 15:15, Saul claims that "the people spared the best of the sheep and of the oxen."

Again in verse 1 Samuel 15:21, he says, "But the people took of the spoil, sheep and oxen, the best of the things devoted to destruction."

When Samuel pressed King Saul as to why he disobeyed God's command, he does not take responsibility as Commander-in-Chief of Israel. Instead, he casts the blame upon those under him. He blamed "the people" instead.

This is unbelievable because, as we saw earlier, Saul was a tyrant of a leader. Earlier, he told his troops not to eat during an entire battle or he would kill them. And his troops were quaking in their sandals in fear.

It is inconceivable that Saul's troops would openly disobey his direct order. If Saul ordered his troops to kill all the livestock, they wouldn't have ignored that command. The only reason the soldiers spared the livestock and took them home was because Saul ordered them to do so.

But that didn't stop Saul from trying to cast blame on others for his own failure.

4. Try to save face ("spin doctoring").

At this point, King Saul knew that he was caught red-handed and none of his tactics worked on Samuel. It was then, and only then, that King Saul finally admitted his failure to Samuel. In verse 24 Saul says, "I have sinned, for I have transgressed the commandment of the Lord and your words..."

Wow, that must have been so hard for him to say. It reminds me of an episode of the TV classic *Happy Days* where The Fonz had to admit he was wrong. But because of his image of being so cool, he had the most difficult time saying, "I was rrr... rrr... rrr....wrong."

Have you ever noticed how contrite politicians and celebrities are after they are caught? They quickly change their tune when the press has proof of their wrongdoing. They look up with puppy dog eyes into the TV cameras at a press conference. They read a carefully crafted statement written by their publicist. Only then do they admit to their failure. But where was the contrition before the evidence came out?

Emblazoned on my memory is Bill Clinton self-right-eously declaring that he "did not have sexual relations with Ms. Lewinsky!" and Lance Armstrong challenging his accusers to show evidence of his cheating to win Tour de France race. After the evidence truth came out, so did their seemingly contrite admission of guilt.

This is called "spin doctoring." To "spin doctor" something to manipulate the facts of the event to give the public a favorable view of the events.

This is what King Saul attempts to do next. After his admission of guilt, Saul asks for forgiveness. Then he tries to rescue the situation so as not to lose face with the rest of Israel. Samuel knew how serious Saul's sin was and how upset God was, but the people didn't. Saul thought that perhaps he could still sweep this under the rug in the eyes of the people.

In 1 Samuel 15:25, Saul asks Samuel,

> *Now therefore, please pardon my sin and return with me that I may bow before the Lord.*

And again in verse 30, Saul says,

> *I have sinned; yet honor me now before the elders of my people and before Israel, and return with me, that I may bow before the Lord.*

Saul's plan was to convince Samuel to not make his sin public, but to act as if nothing had happened.

Here's my paraphrase:

> *Samuel, I know I messed up. I'm sorry. Please forgive me. But this situation doesn't have to leave this room. Why don't you go with me before the people and act as if none of this ever happened? You can stand next to me and we can even offer a sacrifice to God together. The people will never know what I*

did and they will still honor me. What do you think? Isn't that
a clever idea?

Saul had an excellent publicist who was great at spin
doctoring.

Again, the Prophet Samuel saw right through this
attempt at manipulation. It was at this point that Samuel
left King Saul's side as his advisor and guide. Samuel realized that if Saul didn't have the ability to admit his mistakes,
he would never learn from them. And this made him was a
lost cause as a king.

Sadly, the Bible said that the Prophet Samuel gave up
and walked away from Saul that day.

The Bible describes Samuel's disappointment this way:

> *And Samuel did not see Saul again until the day of his death,*
> *but Samuel grieved over Saul. And the Lord regretted that he*
> *had made Saul king over Israel. (1 Samuel 15:35)*

BLESSABLE REPENTANCE

One of the key characteristics of *blessable* people has to do
with repentance. Often, when we think of the word "repentance" or "repent," positive images do not jump into our
thoughts.

We think of angry people from Westboro holding up
signs that admonish everyone but themselves to repent.

They believe that God is upset at everyone other than themselves.

When I think of repentance, I think of altar calls at youth camp. As a teenager, I had a frustrating pattern of trying to do good, failing, and rededicating my life to Jesus. This was also called repentance.

The Bible word for "repentance" is *metanoia*. That word comes from two separate concepts in the Greek language. *Meta* means "to change." *Noia* is the Greek root word for knowledge or thinking. So, *metanoia* literally means to change your mind or way of thinking. There is nothing more personally powerful than changing your mindset.

When you begin to think differently, you will begin to act differently. Theologians define repentance as "the act of changing your mind that leads to the changing of your behavior or actions."

When discussing the concept of repentance, we usually first think of the moment of salvation. The moment that an unbelieving person recognizes their sin and comes to believe in Jesus for their salvation. It's the moment a sinner decides to turn from their sin and embrace Jesus as Lord and Savior. They turn away from a life of sin towards a life of following Jesus. So, repentance is most closely connected with that initial faith experience. Most church-goers identify repentance as only the initiation rite to become a Christian.

I started going to church when I was a teenager and I worked in Youth Ministry for over a decade. Much of our ministry was focused on getting students to repent. I've attended at least 40 Youth Camps as a teenage camper, a Youth Leader, Camp Director and camp speaker.

The pattern was always the same. The camp planners wouldn't necessary admit this. But much of the focus of these Youth Camps was to get teenagers to repent of whatever sins and bad behavior they have been involved in. That's how most of these camps measured their effectiveness. They counted how many teens walked down the aisle to repent from their sin and rededicate their lives to Jesus. It usually happened on what I jokingly call "Cry Night."

My two teenage kids recently went to a Youth Camp. I wasn't involved in the planning of this camp, but I wanted to go for a visit and see how they were doing. So I went to the store and bought some snacks to take to my kids. Yes, I'm a cool dad. I knew that Oreos, Cup O'Noodles, and beef jerky were very valuable items at Youth Camp since they act as currency, much like cigarettes do in prison.

When I got up to the camp, I saw my daughter and asked her how camp was going and if she was having a good time. She said that the camp was amazing!

I asked her, "So did they have 'Cry Night' yet?"

She was shocked. She said, "How did you know? That was last night. All these kids were crying and going up for prayer."

They always have "Cry Night." It's not a good Youth Camp if you don't make a bunch of teenagers feel guilty and make commitments they can't keep. That's repentance. Sort of.

It that context, repentance is not necessarily a positive thing. If you walked down the aisle to "repent and rededicate your life" it meant that you hadn't been a good boy or girl. You realized that you messed up, and to get back into the club you had to repent. Repentance is what the Prodigal Son did only after he came to his senses.

Having come to faith in this setting, the connotation is that repentance is something you do to get started in your faith. And it's also something you do to return to your faith if you mess up. But repentance isn't something good Christians need to do. This is misguided. Repentance is more than the initiation ritual into Christianity or how prodigals return home.

Martin Luther had a radical view of repentance. When he penned the 95 *Theses* that sparked the Protestant Reformation, he started by talking about repentance. He said, "all of life is to be one of repentance." He said that repentance is not only the way to get started or to come back to your faith in Christ. Luther believed the whole of the Christian life of faith should be characterized by repentance.

Luther believed that true faith in God would result in *continual repentance*. Repentance is the constant changing and reorienting of our minds, attitudes and beliefs towards God. If that is true, a person who desires to be blessed by

God should seek to understand and value repentance as a way of life.

DAVID'S EXAMPLE OF REPENTANCE

David was a great leader, but he had a colossal failure later in his life. His sin of adultery with Bathsheba and his conspiracy in the death of her husband Uriah was one of the darkest episodes in the Bible. I don't want to excuse his behavior, but I also cannot cast too many stones.

We have seen too many influential pastors and leaders fall from grace in very public ways. I personally don't look at these stories with judgment, but as cautionary tales. It makes me sober and aware of my own flesh and sinful tendencies. It drives me to pray, "Lord, please protect me from myself."

David's sin with Bathsheba was terribly tragic. It breaks my heart every time I read it. It is finding out that one of your heroes is flawed. It feels like a betrayal of trust. But even in his sin, David is a role model for the rest of us sinners. When the Prophet Nathan confronted David about his secret sin with Bathsheba, he didn't do what Saul did. David repented. And he did it fully.

He didn't blame others or downplay his culpability or make excuses. He didn't do what Adam did in blaming his wife Eve for his decision to eat the forbidden fruit. No, David accepted full responsibility and owned his failure. He didn't make excuses.

Courageously, David looked his sin and failure in the eye and confronted the evil in his own heart. That is the biggest and scariest enemy we will face. It's not the devil from hell, it's the one in the mirror that continues to haunt us day after day.

David writes out his prayer of confession in Psalm 51. He is broken and contrite. He accepts full responsibility and begs God for mercy. The process of facing his sin pushed him closer to God. His desire to be near God grew. He wanted to experience that joy once again. He acknowledges his regretful and sinful actions. He chooses to repent and learn from his failure.

It is interesting when I hear interviews of athletes or celebrities. Usually these interviews are promotional activities set up by a publicist to promote a new album or movie or line of clothing. So the interviewer usually asks boring softball questions. But occasionally, you get a courageous interviewer who asks some real questions such as, "Is there anything that you have done that you now regret?" Now, we all know these celebrities have made huge mistakes because their relational failures and poor life choices are headline news.

Here's the question I want to hear asked:

If you could, is there anything that you would go back and change? Do you have any regrets?

How would you answer that question? I don't think I have ever heard any of these celebrities say, "Yes, I have lots of regrets. There's lots of things that I would change." No, they never say that, because these wildly successful people are some of the most unaware people on the planet. They absolutely should not be the model of "successful" humanity that they are.

That's one the most important and telling questions that can be asked at a job interview: "Do you have any regrets?" How a candidate answers that question will reveal a great deal about that person. It will show if they are aware of their weakness and the results of their actions. Or if they are so self-centered that they don't notice. Their answer reveals if they are smart enough to acknowledge their mistakes so they can learn from them. As the saying goes, "those who do not learn from history are destined to repeat it."

That is never truer than in the microcosm of our own lives. If we are unaware of the history of our own failures and patterns of sin, we will repeat those failures and patterns over and over. This is where repentance comes in.

Repentance is stopping to acknowledge our transgression. It is investigating the collateral damage we caused. It is examining why we did what we did. Accepting full responsibility and asking for forgiveness. Then making the conscious choice to change and make amends if necessary. That's repentance.

Even in his worst failure, David is a model for us in how he repented. Even though his sin had terrible consequences, David handled it the right way. His repentance allowed him to return to being a person God could once again bless. God blessed David in tremendous ways in the second half of his life. This was even after he dealt with the consequences of his sin. David became very wealthy and had a son named Solomon. It was through Solomon that David's legacy would continue.

David was one of the few people in the Scriptures who understood both the height of being a blessed by God and the depths of becoming *unblessable*. God removed His blessing and His presence from David's life for a season.

We can learn a lot about repentance and confession from David's poem to God. In Psalm 51, we hear his heart-breaking words of confession. These are the words of a man who was once blessed, but has become *unblessable*.

Psalm 51:1-2 says,

> *Have mercy on me, O God, according to your steadfast love; according to your abundant mercy blot out my transgressions. Wash me thoroughly from my iniquity, and cleanse me from my sin!*

David cried out because he finally realized what he lost in becoming *unblessable*:

> *Cast me not away from your presence, and take not your Holy*

Spirit from me. Restore to me the joy of your salvation and uphold me with a willing spirit. (Ps. 51:11-12)

What did David lose? Did he lose his kingdom or riches? Nope. He lost the presence of God in his life. And without the presence of God, he had no more joy and his spirit was dead inside of him. But how does he get it back? What is the pathway to regaining that blessing?

Verse 10 says,

Create in me a clean heart, O God, and renew a right spirit within me.

That, I believe, is one of the secrets to a *blessable* life. A clean heart and a right spirit. David knew that God did not want outward acts of penance, but a deep change of heart.

Verse 16-17 says,

For you will not delight in sacrifice, or I would give it; you will not be pleased with a burnt offering. The sacrifices of God are a broken spirit; a broken and contrite heart, O God, you will not despise.

Repentance is one act that can make an *unblessable* person *blessable* again. In Luke 15, Jesus tells the parable of *The Prodigal Son*. A prodigal refers to a kid who has run away from home. Jesus told this story to illustrate the undying love God has for His children. Even the ones who run away to the big city and squander his blessings with prostitutes.

In his state of rebellion, the prodigal was *unblessable*. But the Father never stopped loving him. The Father wisely showed "tough love" to the son. He didn't condone or enable His son's poor decisions and bad behavior.

The Father let His rebellious son run away and hit rock bottom. If you have loved ones with addiction problems you know exactly how difficult "tough love" really is.

Letting someone you love hit rock bottom is one of the most difficult things to do. But is it also the wise thing to do. If you try to rescue a prodigal during their rebellion, you only enable their behavior. So, the most loving thing to do is what the Father did. He let His son hit rock bottom and "come to his senses" on his own.

This led to the moment of his repentance. The prodigal son came to his senses and decided to run back home to his Father. This was the decision that made him *blessable* by his Father again. When the Father saw the son running back home, the Father ran to meet him with hugs and kisses and tears.

He hugged His son and said,

My son, you were lost, now you're found. You were dead, now you're alive. Let's celebrate!

The Father then lavishes His son with great blessing. He gives him a robe, a ring, an embrace, a kiss, and a banquet. What did the son do to deserve these blessings? He had no opportunity to make amends or pay his Father back for the money he lost. No, the thing that made him *blessable* again was repentance. He simply came to his senses and ran back home to see his Daddy.

I don't think we can ever outgrow this beautiful message of repentance. It doesn't matter what mess you've made of your life. Stupid decisions that you regret. People you've hurt. Mistakes you've made. Your rebellion may have made you *unblessable*, but repentance can change all that in a moment.

This reminds me of the line in the famous hymn *Come, Thou Fount,* by Robert Robinson: *"Prone to wander, Lord I feel it. Prone to leave the God I love."*

Therefore, repentance was a great gift to us. It's the reset button on my old *Nintendo 64.* It's the mulligan on the golf course. It's the "do over" at the school playground. Repentance "makes all things new" again. It makes us *blessable* again.

THE HABIT OF RENEWING YOUR FAITH

At the church I lead, we celebrate communion each Sunday. For us, it is our way of renewing our faith and commitment to Jesus.

Before we take communion, I encourage the congregation to confess their sin to God and repent. This is something that I do personally each week. As I take the bread and the cup, I confess my sin, repent from them. Then I renew my commitment to following Jesus as my Savior and Lord.

This regular habit of confession and repentance helps me to stay close to God. I helps me make sure I have not drifted too far in my relationship with God.

I am reminded of what Jesus said to the church in Laodicea.

In Revelation 3:20, Jesus says,

> *Behold, I stand at the door and knock. If anyone hears my voice and opens the door, I will come into him and eat with him, and he with me.*

Jesus was giving this invitation to a church of saved people but who allowed their faith to become "lukewarm." Somehow, these lukewarm Christians managed to lock Jesus outside of their lives. There's a party inside but Jesus is outside knocking at the door. If I'm honest with myself, I would have to admit that in the course of my average week I often manage to lock Jesus outside of my life. I don't do it intentionally. Jesus somehow gets pushed out as I pursue my own goals and desires.

The habit of regular, at the very least weekly, confession and repentance helps me to stay close to God. If your church doesn't observe communion each week, you can create your own habit of renewing your faith by confession and repentance on your own.

SUMMARY

We're all going to mess up and fail from time to time. We're going to sin and disobey God. No one is perfect.

A *blessable* person isn't a perfect person. If being blessed required perfect obedience to God, we would all be hopeless. One of the things that separates a *blessable* person from an *unblessable* one isn't perfection but what they do after they sin and fail God.

What do you do after you fail? Do you deny, blame, or make excuses? Or do you readily confess and repent? Become familiar with repentance. Continual repentance should be a way of life. Make it a habit in your life. Don't go a week without renewing your faith and repenting of your sin. Repentance is one of the key characteristics of a *blessable* life.

Chapter 9

GRATITUDE

BLESSABLE CHARACTERISTIC #7

THE UNGRATEFULNESS OF SAUL

S aul was an ungrateful person. This characteristic comes out in his anger and rash decisions. He isn't thankful for what God has done in his life. You never hear him thanking and praising God.

Ungrateful people are rarely able to see how much God has already blessed them. They whine and complain about the prayers that God has not yet fulfilled. They have a skewed portrait of themselves. They're always the star of their own movie and the hero of every story they tell.

Becoming a thankful person isn't something that happens overnight. But it's a character quality that we all can develop. Ungrateful people are cancers in any community or group. No one wants to be around people who complain all the time. But gratitude is a superpower. It unlocks some of God's greatest blessings we can experience here on earth: contentment and joy. It's impossible for an ungrateful person to experience contentment and joy.

I can't prove that gratitude is the cause of contentment and joy. But it's obvious those three like to hang out a lot. Gratitude, contentment, and joy are three amigos. They go together like peas and carrots. Like peanut butter and jelly. Like milk and cookies. Like Shaq and Kobe (well, at least for a couple of years).

You know what I mean. Gratitude, contentment, and joy are inseparable. They are linked. Where you see one, you're going to find the others. Who does that fool *Ungrateful* hang with? His homies are *Complaining* and *Bitterness*. You don't want to run with that crew. They're bad news. Nothing but trouble. Stay away from them.

BLESSABLE GRATITUDE

Who would you want to bless more? A grateful person or an ungrateful one? That's easy, right? No one wants to be generous to an ungrateful, thankless complainer.

This is one of the reasons God chose to bless David. He was a person who was full of gratitude. He never forgot what God did for him.

Gratitude is one of the most transformative qualities a person can have. The Bible says that gratitude is the fruit of a life that is rooted and built upon the Gospel.

Colossians 2:6-7 says,

Therefore, as you received Christ Jesus the Lord, so walk in him, rooted and built up in him and established in the faith, just as you were taught, abounding in thanksgiving.

The Apostle Paul tells us to "give thanks in all circumstances." Gratitude is simply the state of being truly thankful. It is hard, if not impossible, to be a thankful and a complaining, whining person at the same time.

The opposite of gratitude is being ungrateful. I think that calling someone "ungrateful" is one of the worst things you can say. An ungrateful person is negative, and self-centered, and unaware.

DAVID'S EXAMPLE OF GRATITUDE

We should follow David's example and develop a heart of gratitude. So how do we do that? How can you develop a heart of gratitude? David shows us how. His Psalms and prayers are filled with clues about how to become more thankful.

Let's look at one of his recorded prayers. In 1 Chronicles 17, God makes a promise to David. This is called the Davidic Covenant. God promises to establish and bless David's family with the royal lineage. Even though God denies David's request to allow him to build the Temple, God promises David that his son will have the privilege to build the Temple.

As soon as David hears God's promise, he runs into his

private quarters and offers prayers of praise and thanksgiving to God.

This prayer is recorded in 1 Chronicles 17:16-21.

Who am I, O Lord God, and what is my house, that you have brought me thus far? And this was a small thing in your eyes, O God. You have also spoken of your servant's house for a great while to come, and have shown me future generations, O Lord God!

And what more can David say to you for honoring your servant? For you know your servant. For your servant's sake, O Lord, and according to your own heart, you have done all this greatness, in making known all these great things.

There is none like you, O Lord, and there is no God besides you, according to all that we have heard with our ears. And who is like your people Israel, the one nation on earth whom God went to redeem to be his people, making for yourself a name for great and awesome things, in driving out nations before your people whom you redeemed from Egypt?

This prayer is like many other of David's recorded prayers. When you compare David's prayers of thanksgiving, you'll find they share some common elements. His prayers can help us learn what we need to develop a heart of gratitude.

FIVE ELEMENTS OF GRATITUDE

From this prayer of thanksgiving, we can learn a lot about the elements of gratitude. I want to highlight five essential elements of gratitude.

Gratitude Element #1 - Recognition

David sees and notices everything that God has done for him. Big and small. He acknowledges them and thanks God for each of them.

In verse 16, David says, "this was a small thing in your eyes, O God." In verse 19, he says, "you have done all these great things."

This is the first step to growing a heart of gratitude. You need to open your eyes and recognize what God has already done. You can't be thankful for what you don't notice.

It's so easy to take our blessings for granted. Children are especially guilty of this. They take their parents for granted until they move out and realize that washing your own clothes sucks. They don't realize how much they've been blessed until they get kicked off the family wireless plan. (Yeah, now you know why I keep telling you to stop using the wireless data. That stuff ain't free!)

In verse 16, David acknowledges that God "has brought me thus far." David doesn't take credit for any of his accomplishments. But he acknowledges God's hand of favor and blessing the whole way. That it was God who got him to his place of prominence.

The first step to growing a heart of gratitude is to take notice of what God has already blessed you with. Health, shelter, freedom, family, friends, salvation, provision, wireless plan someone else pays for, etc.

Here's a potentially life-changing suggestion: Make a list of all the things you have that came from God's hands and not your own. Check that. God created your hands too, so everything you earned with your hands also came from God. Write those things down too.

Once you recognize how much God has already blessed you with, you're on your way to developing a heart of gratitude.

Gratitude Element #2 - Humility

We talked about humility in an earlier chapter, so I won't belabor the point too much. But it would be impossible to read one of David's prayers and not notice his humble heart.

He constantly refers to himself as "the Lord's servant."

In verse 16, he starts off his praise of thanksgiving by asking this question of God:

Who am I, O LORD God, and what is my house, that you have brought me thus far?

While David knew he was greatly blessed by God, he still remained amazed that God would choose him. David knew he didn't deserve God's blessings. He never forgot that he was just a skinny, young shepherd boy when God chose him to become the King of Israel. His prayers were filled with gratitude. But it begins with David asking, "Who am I that you chose me?"

Humility leads to gratitude. Whereas pride leads to ungratefulness. Be humble.

Gratitude Element #3 - Memory

One key ingredient to a thankful heart is a good memory. It's not enough to be able to recognize what God is now doing in your life. You need the ability to remember what God has already done in the past.

David had a good memory. He cataloged God's blessings in his writings.

In verses 20-21, he writes:

> *There is none like you, O LORD, and there is no God besides you, according to that we have heard with our ears... great and awesome things, in driving out nations before your people whom you redeemed from Egypt.*

In that one sentence, David remembers and summarizes everything that God did in Exodus and Joshua. David didn't forget what God had done in the past. He remembered the stories of God's blessings and favor in the past.

Why is it so easy for us to forget what God has done?

I often hear the forgetfulness of believers in their anxious prayers. These believers nervously and doubtfully pray timid prayers for God's help with a particular situation in their lives. Their prayers are weak and full of anxiety. This is because they have forgotten how God answered their prayers during their last personal crisis. Their poor memory of God's past faithfulness makes them anxious.

The prayers offered by believers who remember God's faithfulness sound different. These prayers are full of gratitude, trust, and anticipation. These saints speak to God with love and joy. They remember how God lovingly answered their prayers in the past. They cherish what He has already done in their lives.

A good memory of God's faithfulness will help to develop a heart of gratitude.

Gratitude Element #4 - Anticipation

I was going to use the word "hope" to describe this concept, but I wanted a stronger word. Even though "hope" is optimistic, that optimism isn't assured. So let's talk about anticipation instead.

David's heart of gratitude contained a sense of anticipation. He believed God's promises and eagerly awaited their day of fulfillment. He was like a kid on Christmas Eve after

a good report card. He can't go to sleep because of the anticipation of what Christmas morning promises.

God promised to bless David's house and allow his son
Solomon to build the Temple. This was everything David
was hoping for. Now that God had made this promise,
David's hope became anticipation. He anticipated and
prepared for God to fulfill His promise.

Our heart of gratitude is not only based on what God
has done in the past, or what He is now doing. It is also
based on the anticipation that God will keep His promises
to us in the future. We know that our hopes won't all be
fulfilled in this earthly life. But even though many of
God's promises are future and heavenly, they are no less
assured.

Peter reminds us that we have "an inheritance that is
imperishable, undefiled, and unfading, kept in heaven for
you" (1 Peter 1:4). A heart of gratitude is full of a hope that is
so strong it creates anticipation.

The most joyful and mature Christians pray with a
unique sense of anticipation. When they pray, they sometimes thank God ahead of time for things He has not
done yet.

They pray,

Lord, I thank you ahead of time for how you're going to resolve
this situation I'm currently in. I don't know what you're going
to do, but I know you're going to do something. So, I thank you

ahead of time while I eagerly anticipate your answer to this prayer. Amen.

That's a prayer filled with faith, joy, hope, and gratitude. That's how I try to pray today. Maybe you should try it too.

Gratitude Element #5 - Words

A heart of gratitude will express itself in words. You can't help it. The Bible says that "out of the overflow of the heart, the mouth speaks." If you are truly thankful for God's blessings in your life, you can't hold it in. You're going to have to tell someone. David couldn't hold it in either. That's why he wrote so many Psalms.

This is what Mary does when Gabriel tells her she will give birth to the Messiah.

She runs up the hill and twirls around like Julie Andrews in *The Sound of Music* singing the Magnificat:

My soul magnifies the Lord, and my spirit rejoices in God my Savior, for He has looked on the humble estate of His servant. (Luke 1:46-48)

Gratitude turns into praise when you use words. While it's good to be thankful in your heart, it's better to say, "thank you" with your words.

If you want to grow a thankful heart, learn to use your

words to express your gratitude in words to God. Many people have difficulty praying out loud or in the company of others. That's okay. The way I learned how to pray was by writing out my prayers longhand. The best thing I've done for my faith was to develop the habit of keeping a journal of my prayers.

I wrote out everything. I unloaded my frustrations on God. I told Him what I was angry about. I expressed my doubts. And mostly, I kept a record of my prayer requests and how God answered them. My journals are filled with pages and pages that expressed my gratitude to God in words.

I literally have over 50 prayer journals sitting in boxes in my garage. It's a record of my relationship with God and my faith development. Perhaps I'll pass these journals on to my kids so they can get a better picture of who I am. (Of course, I'll have to hide the journals from the early 90's because I was having relational issues with a girl that will remain nameless. Don't worry, it wasn't as bad as Bathsheba. I was just young, insecure, and overly dramatic.)

So, use words. Words are good. Words magically turn your feelings of gratitude into praise that honor God. Selecting the right words will clarify your feelings of gratitude.

PREACHING THE GOSPEL TO YOURSELF

Here's one simple suggestion that will help increase your sense of gratitude. If you regularly do this one, it will make a bigger difference in your faith than anything else I can think of. This is my suggestion: Preach the Gospel to yourself on a regular basis. Develop a habit of reminding yourself of the Bad News and the Good News of the Gospel.

There seems to be a correlation between humility and gratitude. Thankfulness comes from realizing that you don't deserve anything. That's why meditating on the Gospel is so important. Colossians 2:6-7 say that when we are "rooted" in the teaching of the Gospel, the result will be a life "abounding in thanksgiving." Gratitude will overflow our hearts. Why is that? Why does being rooted in the soil of the Gospel result in gratitude?

The Gospel helps us stay grounded in our relationship with God. Learn to preach the Gospel to yourself. It will make all the difference in the world.

The Gospel is Good and Bad

What exactly is the Gospel? The Gospel is the good news that God has sent His Son Jesus to save us. But before you can fully appreciate the Gospel, you must realize that before it is good news, there is bad news. I think too many times we don't realize the context in which the Good News occurs. The Good News is only good because the bad news is so bad. Without the context of the bad news, we can't fully appreciate the good news.

For example, imagine if I run up to you and say,

> *Wow, I have such good news for you. You're going to be so excited and thank me. I really saved your bacon. I saved your car from being towed away today. You had all these unpaid parking tickets, but I paid them for you.*

If that was the first time you heard about the parking tickets, you would respond skeptically. "What are you talking about? What parking tickets? I don't have any unpaid parking tickets."

However, if I told you the bad news first, then the good news, your response would be much different.

> *Hey, I got some bad news for you. The parking enforcement officers came and they were going to give you a parking ticket. They ran your plates and found out that you have a bunch of unpaid parking tickets. It added up to over a thousand dollars. They called a tow truck over to impound your car.*
>
> *But I ran out and asked them what was going on. I asked them if there was any way I could stop the car from being impounded. He said that if I paid off the parking tickets, they wouldn't tow it. So, here's the good news. I paid off your parking tickets and stopped your car from getting towed.*

If I told you that information, in that order, your response would be different. I believe one of the reasons that Christians are not very thankful is that we don't understand the depth of the Gospel. We hear the Gospel presented to us as "God loves you and has a wonderful plan for your life." When we start there, it is implied that the reason God loves us and wants to bless us must be because we are such great people.

The Bad News of the Gospel

The Bad News of the Gospel is that we are all sinners. Every single person that has ever existed is a sinner. The Bible clearly says that "there is none righteous, no not one... all have sinned and fall short of God's glory" (Romans 3:10, 23). Sin is the breaking of God's moral law. We constantly sin against God's law in our words, thoughts, and deeds. We sin both consciously and unconsciously.

And the Bad News gets worse. The Bible tells us that "the wages of sin is death" (Romans 6:23). What is a "wage"? A wage is what you earn for yourself when you do a job. If you work for the wage of $10 an hour and you work for 5 hours, you earn for yourself $50. That's what you can expect to receive. That's what you have coming to you. That's yours.

So what does it mean, "the wages of sin is death"? That means that every time you sin (which is constantly) you are earning for yourself the wage of death. And it's not just physical death.

The Bible also talks about spiritual death and eternal death. Spiritual death is when our souls are separated from a relationship with God. This is what happened to Adam and Eve in the garden. God said that if they ate of the forbidden fruit they would surely die that day.

However, they didn't die physically; they died spiritually. Their eyes were opened to their nakedness. The emotion of shame overcame them for the first time. So, they hid from each other and God behind fig leaves. This is spiritual death.

When spiritual death meets with physical death it will result in eternal death. When a spiritually dead person dies physically, that state of death becomes permanent. That person's eternal soul will continue to live on in separation from God. This state of eternal death is commonly known as hell.

The Bible teaches that Hell is a literal place of punishment that God created for the devil. Although the Bible and Jesus speak often about eternal death, it is often done in metaphoric terms. Jesus calls it "outer darkness" and "Gehenna" and a place where "the worms never die and the fire is never quenched." "Gehenna" is a literal place in the city of Jerusalem. The word "Gehenna" is the transliteration for the neighboring "Valley of Hinnom." Hinnom is the valley just outside the walls of the old city of Jerusalem. It was the garbage dump and landfill for the city during Jesus' day.

This is not an uncommon occurrence. Even in our day,

we have millions living in the garbage dumps of Myanmar, Bangladesh, Manilla, Jakarta, New Delhi, Kathmandu, and Guizhou. When Jesus said that a person who is not in right relationship with God will be cast into Gehenna, everyone knew what He meant. That's what He was referring to when He said there the worms do not die and the fires are never quenched. Imagine all the maggots and flies around the rotting and burning trash in that landfill.

Imagine the stench of the constantly burning garbage. That is what Jesus says is what a life eternally separated from God is like. And that is the destination for every person who is spiritually dead after their physical lives end. That is eternal death. That is bad news.

But wait, there's more. Sorry folks, the bad news gets even worse. Not only are we sinners with a reservation for an eternal stay in a dumpster fire, but there's nothing we can do to fix the situation ourselves. We think that we can figure our way out of the messes we create.

Like G.I. Joe reminded the children of the 80s, "Knowing is half the battle." But knowing that we are sinners doesn't solve the problem. Because there are no good works that we can do to fix the problem we are in. Even if we tried hard to live a perfectly righteous and sinless life from this point on, our good behavior cannot atone for our past sin. Good behavior only works to prevent us from incurring new debts of spiritual death.

So, the bad news includes that our good works don't work. They don't. We cannot fix our problem with sin, because we are the problem. There is no amount of good deeds we can do to atone for our sin. It doesn't matter how many old ladies you walk across the street, volunteer hours you give, or dollars you donate. Your good works won't work to atone for your past sin.

The Good News of the Gospel

Now that we are all thoroughly depressed, I have good news for you. It's really great news! The good news is only really, really good when we fully understand and appreciate how really bad the bad news is.

The good news is that even though we are sinners destined for eternal death, God has never stopped loving us. He loves us so completely. For some reason we can't comprehend, God delights and takes pleasure in us. Yes, our Creator loves us! That's the primary message of the entire Bible.

The Bible is a story of a loving Father whose children were deceived into rebelling against Him. This Father goes on an eternal quest to bring His children back home. That's the unifying story of the whole Bible. You are loved by God, even in your sin and rebellion. God wants to bring you back home.

For God to bring you back home, He had to pay for the debts of the sin that you incurred. Remember, the wages of sin is death. So God had to send someone to be your substitute. Someone had to die for you to live.

In His wisdom and grace, God sent His Son Jesus, the second person of the Trinity, to be your substitute. Jesus lived a perfect life, a life that you couldn't live. And at the appointed time, He allowed Himself to be arrested and punished. He was killed by crucifixion, not for His sin, but for ours.

Jesus came to earth to trade places with us. He came to be our substitute. He took our place on the Cross, so that we can have his seat next to His Father in heaven. "O the bliss of this glorious thought!" Horatio Spafford exclaimed when thinking about what Jesus did for us. The best part of the good news is that what Jesus did for us is a gift. Free. Not cheap, but free.

This gift was the most expensive gift ever given because it cost Jesus His life. But to us it is free. As with any gift, you cannot earn it or pay for it. But you must receive it.

This is the good news – The Gospel. It is news of the free gift of Jesus' death on the Cross to atone for our sin. This gift is offered to all who are willing to take it. Good news of great joy! Amazing grace, how sweet the sound that saved a wretch like me!

The Gospel, the bad news and the good news, is the soil that Christians need to be rooted in. And when we grow our lives out of this rich soil, it naturally produces the rich fruit of gratitude. How can it not?

It is inconsistent and illogical for Christians to be ungrateful and full of complaining. Many so-called followers of Jesus struggle to be thankful because they don't think that God has done enough for them. They think that God owes them a bigger slice of the American Dream. In their hearts, they harbor contempt for God and say, "God, if you can't give me what I want, why do I need you around?"

SUMMARY

It shouldn't be, but gratitude has become a rare superpower today. Complaining and griping and criticism are far too common, especially when things don't go our way.

Gratitude makes you into a more *blessable* person. The best way to develop gratitude as a characteristic in your life is to remind yourself of the Gospel. If you can't be thankful for the Gospel, you'll never be thankful for anything.

Learn to preach the Gospel to yourself regularly, if not daily. Remind yourself of the bad news of your sin. Then remind yourself of the amazing good news of what Jesus has done for you. If you make this a habit in your life, it will change you and give you a heart of gratitude.

I am so grateful for many things that God has done in my life. Most of all, I am grateful for the Gospel. I remind myself of it daily.

What are you grateful for? Thank Him. You'll be blessed if you do.

CONCLUSION

David's life is an example of a person we can model ourselves after. He's not perfect. But he has character. And it all starts from his heart for God.

This is where David excels. There is a reason why his prayers, songs and poems have lived on in our hearts today. David's Psalms are so rich because they were written from the heart of a man who was after the heart of God.

For me, the ultimate value of David's life and example is that it serves as an arrow pointing me to Jesus. David was a good man. A flawed person with huge regrets, but a good man. He is a person we can learn from, but I don't think he should be our "role model." However, his life serves to point us to the true hero, which is Jesus.

So, David is not a perfect guy. And that is good news for us who are also imperfect people. We don't have to be perfect to live a life that God deems *blessable*. We will inevitably make mistakes, have regrets, and dark moments of doubt and despair. None of those things preclude us from being blessed by God. Do you want to be blessed by God? Yes, of course. I know I do.

David serves as one of the *Great Cloud of Witnesses* that shout to us that a *blessable* life is possible. You don't have to stand tall and talented like Saul to be blessed. Just focus on living a *blessable* life in pursuit of God. Believe that the God that David pursued is not hiding from you. Actually, He is actively pursuing you too. Jesus is pursuing your heart. Be *blessable*. And, just maybe, you will find that your Father in heaven is far more than willing and eager to open the floodgates of heaven and pour out His blessing upon your life.

This is my encouragement to you. It may seem a bit counter-intuitive, but trust me. And trust the Word of the Blessing God as we have explored it.

Are you ready for it? Here it is: Don't try to be like David. David is not a perfect guy. As they say, "the best of men are still men at best."

David is not perfect. But Jesus is. Don't seek to be David. Seek to find David's God. Become a person who is after God's heart, a truly *blessable* person.

I know if you do that, you'll be blessed!

LET'S STAY CONNECTED

I want to thank you for allowing me to share my thoughts with you. I hope that you this book has been helpful to you.

I would love to connect with you. Check out my website.

I have a bunch of FREE resources available. There's hours of videos of my teaching, workshops, PDF downloads, and much more.

Here's how you can find me.

My website:
www.thiendoan.net

My Facebook Page:
www.facebook.com/thiendoan.net

CAN I ASK FOR A FAVOR?

Thanks for reading my book. I do have a favor to ask. This is an independently published book and I don't have a marketing department or a big budget for advertisement. The only way this book won't get lost in the digital ether is if you leave a review on Amazon.

It will only take you a minute. You can always go back and edit your review later. Just be honest. So, can you do me a solid and leave me a review on Amazon?

If you're reading the e-book edition, when you turn the page, Kindle will give you the option to rate this book and share your thoughts on Facebook and Twitter.

If you found value in this book, I would appreciate it if you would take a few seconds and click the FIVE STARS icon and share it with your friends. Thank you so much.

Blessings,
Thien

Do you want FREE RESOURCES?

Visit my website:
www.thiendoan.net

Teaching videos
Seminars & Workshops
PDF Downloads
Beta Editions of future books

Made in the USA
Middletown, DE
03 January 2020

82158720R00118